Jim Selley

THE STRUGGLE FOR SUPREMACY
IN THE BALTIC 1600–1725

The Struggle for Supremacy in the Baltic 1600–1725

JILL LISK B.A.

HODDER AND STOUGHTON
LONDON SYDNEY AUCKLAND TORONTO

ISBN 0 340 07995 9

First published 1967
Seventh impression 1984

Printed in Great Britain for Hodder and Stoughton
Educational, a division of Hodder and Stoughton Ltd,
Mill Road, Dunton Green, Sevenoaks, Kent, by
Biddles Ltd, Guildford, Surrey

CONTENTS

MAPS

Chief Timber Ports: ⬆ fir ♀ oak
<u>Riga</u> Hanseatic Towns
－－－ Boundaries of Baltic States
Denmark
Sweden
Poland
Russia
Brandenburg-Prussia

0   100   200   300   400 miles

THE BALTIC REGION AT THE OPENING
OF THE SEVENTEENTH CENTURY

PART I
Europe and the Baltic, 1600–1725

[1] THE BALTIC REGION

The importance of the Baltic region in seventeenth and early eighteenth-century European history is often overlooked and frequently only partly understood. The protracted struggles of the Baltic powers for supremacy, fascinating in themselves, are not fully appreciated without some insight into the way in which they were influenced by, and the nature of their influence upon, the rest of Europe.

The Baltic Sea is bigger than it looks. It extends practically 1,000 miles from the extreme west to the east. Three narrow outlets, the Sound (which divides modern Denmark and Sweden), the Great Belt and the Little Belt, are the main maritime highways to the North Sea, and just prevent the Baltic Sea from being a very large lake. Tides are measured in inches rather than feet and the water is only slightly salt. The shallowness and freshness of the Baltic account for the ease with which it freezes, a very important fact in the economy of the Baltic powers. In most winters in the seventeenth century the eastern ports were completely iced up and occasionally the western approaches as well. (Thus in 1658 Charles X of Sweden transported a large army across the Belts over the ice.) Vast quantities of fresh water flow into the Baltic from several rivers of great economic and commercial importance. These long navigable rivers, notably the Vistula, the Dvina and the Oder, connect the Baltic with an extensive hinterland, and with other great rivers such as the Rhine, the Weser and the Elbe. Further commercial potentialities of the Baltic Sea are its proximity to the North Sea, its fish resources and its excellent harbourage. The importance of such ports as Danzig and Stettin is constantly brought home in a study of the region during this period.

Situated on or near the shores of the Baltic Sea at the opening of the seventeenth century were a number of states whose rivalry is the subject of this study. Across the narrow outlet to the North Sea lay Denmark, the dominant power in the Baltic. At this time Denmark included Norway, the southern coasts of what is now modern Sweden, and the strategic islands of Gotland, Bornholm and Ösel. Her neighbour, Sweden, ruled Finland and had recently acquired Estonia in the east. (This province, together with Livonia, had originally been conquered by a German Order of Crusading Knights, and when the Order collapsed in the 1550s, Sweden, Russia and Poland quarrelled over the spoils.) There was, as yet, no indication that Sweden would shortly dominate not only the Baltic but much of Germany as well. Russia in 1600 was struggling with Sweden in order to maintain her very narrow outlet to the Baltic on the Gulf of Finland. She was soon to lose it and be cut off from the sea for a century. In regaining her 'window' to the west Russia was to bring about the dramatic downfall of Sweden. In the south-eastern corner of the Baltic sprawled the vast state of Poland. She had temporarily acquired Livonia but would gain no more in the seventeenth century. In fact this once powerful nation was doomed to become a prey to her neighbours, Sweden, Russia and Brandenburg. Along the southern Baltic coasts lay several other states which were part of the Holy Roman Empire – Holstein, Mecklenburg and Pomerania. More important than these in the seventeenth century was another, Brandenburg, the Elector of which was also from 1618 the Duke of East Prussia (for a time under the suzerainty of Poland), and was thus directly concerned in Baltic affairs. Brandenburg herself was soon to gain territory along the German Baltic coast in the shape of Eastern Pomerania. Finally, no brief description of the Baltic region would be complete without some mention of the important Hanse towns. By 1300 groups of towns in northern Europe such as Hamburg, Lübeck, Danzig and Wisby, had built up an extensive commerce and come together in a somewhat loose and ill-defined organization called the Hanseatic League. The League was to number nearly one hundred towns and to dominate northern commerce for more than two centuries. By the beginning of the seventeenth century much of their trade had been lost to others, particularly the Dutch, but these trading communities were still a considerable factor in Baltic politics.

In the early seventeenth century, at the time of the Thirty Years' War, Sweden exerted a decisive influence on the course of European affairs and in fact seemed on the point of reorganizing central Europe. Towards the end of the century two other northern powers, Russia and Prussia, forced the rest of Europe to take notice of their interests and demands for the first time. Until this time Brandenburg-Prussia, a scattered, backward state, was of little account, and Russia, regarded as Asiatic and barbaric, did not figure in the calculations of European statesmen. Only in Baltic politics did these states count at all, and even there they were of little importance. However, by 1721, Prussia having been raised to the status of a kingdom, and Russia quite clearly the strongest power in the north, could no longer be ignored. But what of the Baltic and Europe during the rest of the century? G. N. Clark[1] points out that the Baltic can be seen to function separately from the rest of Europe, and indeed the struggle for power in western Europe and the contest for supremacy in the Baltic continued independently for considerable periods. Nevertheless important overlapping occurred and, when a close examination is made of the numerous occasions upon which the European powers considered it necessary to intervene in the Baltic throughout the period, it becomes clear that the region was of great importance to them.

The great powers of seventeenth-century Europe often found

1. G. N. Clark, *The Seventeenth Century*, Oxford University Press (paperback) (London, 1960).

valuable allies among the northern nations for their political and dynastic schemes. Occasionally the Baltic was regarded as a field of conquest, and the ambitions of the Habsburgs in the early seventeenth century led to repercussions resulting in Sweden's dramatic 'foray' into European politics. French policy during the whole period is more readily understood when the significance of the northern powers in France's anti-Habsburg plans is made clear. Furthermore the maritime struggle between England and the Dutch and between the Dutch and the French during this century was very closely connected with the Baltic. But first the fundamental importance of the Baltic in the economy of seventeenth-century Europe must be clearly understood.

[2] THE ECONOMIC IMPORTANCE OF THE BALTIC TO SEVENTEENTH-CENTURY EUROPE

The Baltic states were not only the main European source of timber, required in vast quantities for shipbuilding (and in particular of those trees most suitable for masts), but also of such naval necessities as tar and pitch (preservatives for the structure of ships and their canvas) and hemp and flax for sails, canvas, rope and anchor cables. In addition this region supplied the rest of Europe with the bulk of its grain, copper and iron-ore.

Demand for all these commodities increased steadily during the seventeenth century. Europe was growing more prosperous; economic life was intensifying and becoming more widespread; military, naval and mercantile activity speeded up. In particular the Anglo-Dutch war of 1652-4 opened a new epoch in naval matters and the maritime powers (England, the United Provinces and later France) began to build up large navies while the Baltic powers constructed forces on a rather smaller scale. Increasing commercial rivalry between the maritime powers is illustrated in their attempts to gain privileges in the northern trade and outdo each other. As yet the great timber industry of North America was undeveloped and the timber that did appear from that part of the world was despised as inferior. In the following century this situation changed and the maritime powers, relying on their American colonies, were not as dependent on the Baltic region. But in the seventeenth century the Baltic was an indispensable source of supply. With the general growth of industry and the expansion of towns, the western powers also required increased supplies of corn from the lands of the eastern Baltic. Moreover Sweden had established a near-monopoly not only of copper, essential for the manufacture of armaments and coinage, but also of high-quality iron-ore. By far the greatest consumer of Swedish iron was England who became particularly dependent upon it during the later years of the period when English wood supplies (for smelting) became exhausted. In return for all these products, timber, corn and minerals, the Baltic presented an ever-increasing market for British and Flemish textiles, French and German wines, and innumerable goods from the New World and the East.

It is thus evident that the maritime powers had the greatest interest in, and the most to lose by, any major disruption of the balance of power in the Baltic. But at least during the earlier part of the period, Spain and the Empire pursued active policies in that region.

[3] HABSBURG POLICY IN THE BALTIC

In 1600 Spain was still regarded as the leading power in the world. Relations with the Austrian branch of the Habsburgs were very close and constantly strengthened by intermarriage. Spain had large resources, was dominant in Italy and religiously united. Contemporaries did not foresee the rapid decay of that great nation during the seventeenth century. At the opening of the period she was the first naval power in Europe, and was trading with the Baltic for masts, timber and naval stores. She adopted a copper coinage in 1599 and thus needed large quantities of the Swedish mineral. Moreover during the long struggle with the Dutch both sides saw the importance of controlling the Sound. The Spanish Ambassador in Sweden suggested to Philip II that he should capture Elsinore and Hälsingborg, and thus control Dutch trade, in the hope of persuading the United Provinces to sue for peace. After the Twelve Years' Truce of 1609 (between Spain and the United Provinces) Spain still showed great interest in the Baltic. She was always conscious of the tremendous volume of Dutch trade which went through the Sound, and cherished hopes of obtaining, from Denmark or Poland, a Baltic port from which to strike at the Dutch.

The Imperial Habsburgs were not without pretensions to sovereignty over the Baltic Sea. During the Thirty Years' War the idea of challenging the Dutch by means of a Spanish-German trading company was mooted. Poland, it was hoped, would join. Another current idea was that a combined Habsburg-Hanseatic fleet would seize control of the Baltic from the Protestant powers. Indeed it was the imminent capture by the Imperialists of the German Baltic coastline which finally brought Sweden into the Thirty Years' War.

But Habsburg ambitions in the Baltic failed and after the Thirty Years' War neither the Spaniards nor the Austrians were able to intervene decisively in the north. Spain was declining seriously and her navy had practically disappeared. Her colonial trade was more and more quarrelled-over by the English and the Dutch while the rise of France and the following Franco-Spanish conflict led to the fall of Spain in 1659 at the Peace of the Pyrenees. Moreover, the great effort made by the Empire during the Thirty Years' War to create a centralized monarchy and subdue the princes was by 1648 clearly in vain. After that date, as Barraclough points out: 'The Empire was a meaningless historical survival, Germany a geographical expression'.[2] The dignity of the Empire indeed remained in Habsburg hands, and the large

2. G. Barraclough, *The Origins of Modern Germany*, Blackwell (Oxford, 1947).

hereditary lands belonging to the Austrian monarchy meant that the latter was a force to be reckoned with. In fact, the second half of the seventeenth century saw a distinct revival in the power of that House, in resistance to the Turk, in subduing Hungary, and in opposing Louis XIV. But Austrian influence was turning more and more to the east and the gainers in central and northern Europe were the German princes and, above all, France. For the most part, subsequent Habsburg interest in the Baltic was confined to a fear that Sweden, the strongest northern state after the Thirty Years' War, might dominate Catholic Poland or extend her power even further. The general devastation of Germany after the war led to the domination of trade and commerce by foreigners, especially the Dutch. The Hanseatic cities were greatly impoverished and the great centres of European trade shifted to the Atlantic coast.

[4] THE DUTCH AND THE BALTIC

To the Dutch, the Baltic was of paramount importance throughout the seventeenth century. Baltic trade was, they declared, the basis of their whole commerce, for they fully realized that, once the naval supplies from the Baltic were shut off, their enormous trade in the Indies, South Seas and elsewhere was doomed. Throughout the period, despite fierce competition, the large majority of the ships passing through the Sound were Dutch. The United Provinces were almost completely dependent on imported timber as they had few trees, and the grain which they obtained from the great plains of Poland and Russia was regarded as their 'mother commerce'. In 1658 the British Minister at The Hague wrote of the Dutch and the importance of their Baltic or 'East Sea' trade:

This trade of the East Sea is one of the greatest mysteries in trade, they venting there what they bring out of the east, south and west;

and again, supplying other countries with commodities of that sea
. . . and although their Spanish and East Indy trade be richer, yet
the destroying of this trade is also the destroying of those other.[3]

Gradually the Dutch built up a huge merchant marine and to a
large extent both England and France became dependent upon
it for essentials of naval construction and other vital commodities.
Dutch ships were built at a third the cost of the English and the
United Provinces maintained a low rate of interest. Estimates
vary as to the size of the Dutch fleet; Colbert considered it
numbered about 15,000 to 16,000 ships out of a possible world
total of 20,000. Another estimate puts it at twice the number of
the French, English and German merchant fleets put together,
and Sir William Petty, a contemporary economist, suggests that
it was twice that of the English and nine times that of the French.

The Dutch early established their supremacy in Baltic trade.
In 1600, we are told, between 800 and 900 ships left Amsterdam
in three days carrying goods to and from the Baltic. Zaandam
became the centre of the European timber trade, and shipbuilding prospered at Enkhuizen, Hoorn and other towns on the
Zuider Zee. In the valuable Russian trade there was a long
struggle between the Dutch and the English, but it ended during
the seventeenth century in a victory for the former. Archangel
had been founded under Dutch influence and it has been estimated
that ten times as many Dutch as English ships visited that port.
The Dutch had strong colonies also in Moscow and Riga. In
Sweden the port of Göteborg was founded by the Dutch under a
certain Abraham Cabelliau, an Amsterdam merchant, and continued for years to be practically a Dutch town. Moreover during
this period the Dutch largely controlled the iron and copper
mines of Sweden.

3. Quoted by Robert Albion, *Forests and Sea Power*, Harvard University Press
(Cambridge, Mass., 1926).

[5] ENGLAND AND THE BALTIC

Commercial rivalry between the Dutch and the English was intense throughout the century. In the Baltic the English were determined to keep the Sound open to trade, and great efforts were made to destroy Dutch dominance. Seeley wrote:

In those days, and after those days, for more than a century, it was a matter of life and death for England that no power . . . should acquire the power of shutting the Baltic. On this principle our Baltic policy almost exclusively rested.[4]

Imperial designs on the Baltic during the Thirty Years' War were recognized as dangerous. Sir Thomas Roe wrote to the Prince of Orange, December 1628:

The loss of the free trade of the Baltique Sea is more dangerous to the Kingdome of England and to the United Provinces than any other prosperity of the House of Austria, being the indys of the materialls of shipping, and, consequently both of their strength, riches and subsistence. There is no counsell so necessarye and so pressive as the consideration of the meanes to preserve it in liberty, which being subjugated to the Emperor, the Hanse towns must of necessitye submitt to him.[5]

But what perturbed the English most was that early in the seventeenth century they had become dependent upon the Dutch for essentials of naval construction.

During the period of the Commonwealth there was a striking increase in English naval power. The foundations had been laid with the ship-money fleets of Charles I but the great development took place between 1649 and 1660. In these years 207 new ships were added to the navy, and it has been estimated that 16,000 men were employed in contrast to the 3,000 or 4,000 of Charles I's time. Moreover men more closely in touch with commercial matters were now in control of affairs. Similar changes

4. J. R. Seeley, *The Growth of British Policy*, Cambridge University Press (Cambridge, 1895).
5. Quoted by Charles E. Hill, *The Danish Sound Dues and the Command of the Baltic*, Duke University Press (Durham, N. Carolina, 1926).

were occurring in the United Provinces and as a result the rivalry between the two nations grew rapidly until it culminated in open war. English timber was in very short supply and fear for trade in the Baltic was instrumental in bringing about the Navigation Act of 1651 which prohibited any foreign country (principally, of course, the Dutch) from bringing goods to England unless that country actually produced the goods conveyed. At the same time bounties were introduced on the production of naval stores in the hope that they would free England, at least to some degree, from dependence on Dutch-carried Baltic supplies.

During the first Anglo-Dutch War, 1652-4, the English admiral Blake was ordered to take the fleet north and, among other things, 'interrupt and disturb' the Dutch Eastland (Baltic) trade, at the same time protecting that of the Commonwealth. The rival Baltic powers, Denmark and Sweden, joined, as usual, opposite sides in the struggle and in 1653 Denmark (an ally of the Dutch) closed the Sound against the English who consequently found themselves cut off from their main source of timber, tar, hemp and other vital naval supplies. In a speech of January 1658 Cromwell warned against the Dutch menace:

If they can shut us out of the Baltic Sea and make themselves masters of that, where is your trade? Where are the materials to preserve your shipping? Where will you be able to challenge any right by sea or justify yourselves against a foreign invasion on your own soil? Think upon it, this is in design.[6]

In the following year, as part of the general efforts of the maritime powers to keep the peace in the Baltic, Richard Cromwell sent the English fleet to the Sound: distrust between the English and the Dutch grew and once again very nearly led to war. The debates in Parliament at this time reveal very clearly England's Baltic policy. Secretary Thurloe pointed out that

The continuance of war in these parts would infinitely hinder our trade and be of great prejudice to this nation; many of our manufactures being transported and vended thither, many of our materials for shipping and navigation being carried from thence hither. . . . Con-

6. Quoted by Robert Albion, op. cit.

sidering what the issue of this war might be, that the Sound was likely to be put in the hands of those that would exclude the English or put us in such condition, as we should be as bad as excluded; the consequences of which could be the ruin of our shipping, hemp, pitch, tar, cordage and masts, coming all from thence and an obstruction there would endanger our safety. We had experience of this in our war with the Dutch, when the Dane did prohibit our access thither, which put us to great distress, having none of those commodities but what came from our enemies at double rates.[7]

Gradually the volume of English shipping passing through the Sound increased; the 1660 Navigation Act was particularly effective in driving the Dutch out of England's trade with the Baltic. But during the second Anglo-Dutch war, 1665–7, the Sound was again closed to the English and the shortage of naval materials was even more acute. Pepys wrote in his Diary in December 1666:

There is also the very good news come of four New England ships come home safe to Falmouth with masts for the King, which is a blessing mighty unexpected, and without which, if for nothing else, we must have failed next year.

Three weeks later he wrote:

No newes yet of our Gottenburgh fleete; which makes [us] have some fears, it being of mighty concernment to have our supply of masts safe.

During the third Anglo-Dutch War, 1672–4, the timber problem in England was at its worst ever. A letter of March 1673 from a principal timber contractor reveals the difficulty:

The Young Blackcock with New England masts taken by the Dutch 1st of Feb. last; the Great Blackcock with ditto masts taken by Dutch 23 Jan. . . . One of our Gottenburg ships taken when laden and carried to Holland: two other Gottenburg mast ships taken by the Scots . . .[8]

The Anglo-Dutch union of 1689 meant that rivalry between the two nations diminished and the northern powers could no

7. Quoted by Robert Albion, op. cit.
8. Quoted by Robert Albion, op. cit.

longer play off one against the other. But timber shortages remained a serious problem. Robert Albion's study on the importance of forests to sea-power is extremely illuminating and brings
home the vital importance of the Baltic. After the 1680s, supplies
of oak and pine ran out in England and large quantities of timber
were imported from Courland, East Prussia and Scandinavia.
The Navigation Laws were even modified to allow foreign ships
to carry it. Moves were made to acquire larger quantities of
timber from North America and bounties were granted; the one
great disadvantage here was that transatlantic freights were
about three times as high as those of the Baltic. The War of the
League of Augsburg against France, 1689-97, led to further shortages in English shipping; by 1694 it has been estimated that some
4,000 vessels had been lost. Consequently the demand for Baltic
timber became heavier: in 1697 the Board of Trade made an
extensive inquiry into the situation, recommending that England
should turn to America and Ireland.

The Great Northern War, which lasted for two decades until
peace was made in 1721, presented further difficulties. During the
earlier years of the conflict it appeared that the Baltic was in
danger of becoming a Swedish lake, so successfully did Charles
XII of Sweden deal with his numerous attackers. English traders
suffered in particular and the English woollen trade with Sweden
was ruined by Charles's unfriendly measures. In 1703 the Swedes
refused to sell tar to England except as they should see fit. The
British Minister in Stockholm informed his government

That they might see how much it was in the power of the King of
Sweden either to forward the fitting out of the Royal Navy or to
keep it in harbour.[9]

But soon another factor had to be considered. A Russian navy
was growing in the Baltic and after the downfall of Sweden in
1709 it became a serious threat. In 1713 the English Ambassador
at The Hague, Lord Stafford, wrote:

9. Quoted by Robert Albion, op. cit.

Naturally England would never wish to see the Swedish Crown ruined and powerless. England's intention was to maintain the balance between all the powers in the north as it was before.[10]

In 1716 Townshend, the British Secretary of State, remarked:

It is our misfortune at this juncture, by the Knavery of the Muscovites . . . to have our naval magazines so ill-provided with stores, particularly with hemp, that if the fleet of merchantmen, now lading in the Baltick, should by any accident miscarry, it will be impossible for His Majesty to fitt out any ships of war for the next year, by which means the whole navy of England will be rendered perfectly useless.[11]

In short, England's safety depended upon the balance of power in the Baltic and the numerous occasions upon which she sent her fleet to that sea, particularly in the later years of the period, bear witness to her anxiety about the events in the north.

[6] FRANCE AND THE BALTIC

The strongest power in Europe from the time of the Thirty Years' War was France, and for most of the century the Baltic was an essential area in French schemes to encircle and confine the Habsburgs. The usual plan was to form alliances with Turkey, the states of central Europe and Sweden in the north. Thus French statesmen were constantly immersed in negotiations to maintain or bring about peace in the Baltic in order to be free to carry out their plans elsewhere without complications. Sweden was regarded as one of France's greatest assets, and the two countries were allies for long periods in the seventeenth century.

But France was also developing rapidly as a commercial and maritime power and her efforts to establish her position, in opposition mainly to the Dutch, illustrate very well the importance of the Baltic to the rest of Europe. In earlier times France had frequently engaged in northern trade but by the 1620s, when

10. Quoted by Ian Grey, *Peter the Great, Emperor of All Russia*, Hodder (London, 1962).
11. Quoted by J. F. Chance, *George I and the Northern War*, Smith, Elder (London, 1909).

Richelieu assumed power in France, the Dutch monopolized Baltic commerce and the carrying of French goods. It was the Cardinal who endeavoured to alter this situation and bring about direct French participation in Baltic trade. He wrote in his *Political Testament*:

The wealth of the Dutch, who, to tell the truth, are only a handful of folk crammed into a corner of the earth where there are only water and fields, is an example and proof of the advantages of trade which cannot be denied. . . . Although that nation gets from its land only butter and cheese, yet it supplies nearly all the nations of Europe with the greater part of their necessities.

Richelieu continually advocated the development of the navy and merchant marine, and was appalled by France's lack of ships under Henry IV and Louis XIII. Much of Richelieu's work in these matters came to little as a result of internal strife and the Thirty Years' War, but a beginning had been made in building up a French fleet and in extending French commerce in the Baltic. Under his successor, Cardinal Mazarin, trade, commerce and naval matters stagnated; further progress had to wait until Jean-Baptiste Colbert came to power in France in 1661 on Mazarin's death.

Colbert was determined to make France an industrial, commercial, naval and, if possible, a colonial power. He, also, was particularly impressed by the success of the Dutch and constantly strove to break their power by building up the navy and merchant marine, and endeavouring to make France economically self-sufficient. He pointed out that the Dutch had about 16,000 ships carrying the commerce of the world, whereas France had only about 500 or 600. He painted a black picture of the position:

As we have crushed Spain on land, so we must crush Holland at sea. The Dutch have no right to usurp all commerce . . . knowing very well that so long as they are masters of trade their naval forces will continue to increase and make them so powerful that they will be able to assume the role of arbiters of peace and war in Europe and set limits on the King's plans.[12]

12. Quoted by *New Cambridge Modern History*, Vol. V, Chap. IX, Cambridge University Press (Cambridge, 1961).

Under Colbert's guidance French shipping, naval and mercantile, made great strides. He tells us that when he first took office there were only 20 warships in the French navy. By 1671 there were 196 effective vessels, and by 1677 this had increased to 270. Shipbuilding was given a tremendous boost; old harbours were put in order and new ones created. With regard to the mercantile marine, Colbert kept the fifty sous a ton tax on foreign ships which had been instituted by Fouquet, his financial predecessor, and paid bounties of five and six livres a ton for ships used in the Baltic. A survey was made of all French forests near rivers upon which logs would float, and French resources in America were explored. The production of timber, tar, sailcloth and munitions was strongly encouraged. But Colbert was still forced to place large orders for timber in Scandinavia despite the numbers of agents scouring France for forests and compelling their owners to sell to the state. In fact, instead of being able to sell naval stores to other countries as Colbert had forecast, France found herself still dependent on Baltic supplies.

The 'Compagnie du Nord' founded by Colbert in 1669 was a venture dear to his heart. The company was set up with the specific aim of undermining the Dutch hold upon the trade in naval stores and general commerce in the north. (In 1668, out of 200 ships going from the Baltic to France, 111 were Dutch.) The company was to exchange French wine, brandy and salt for naval materials, and was warned to be wary of the Dutch. In a letter of 1669 Colbert declared that the company should regard the latter 'as mortal enemies who would go to any length to ruin them [the French]'. The idea behind the project was a good one but Colbert was never able to rouse much enthusiasm for this or any other company he founded. Moreover it was established at a time when Franco-Dutch rivalry was intense. The latter had the advantage of being in control of the market and used every means to prevent the French from gaining a foothold. But gradually French commerce in the north increased and it played an important part in keeping France in provisions during Louis XIV's long wars. Indeed when it is remembered that France as a naval and commercial power could hardly be said to have existed at all at the beginning of the century, her progress in these matters was clearly considerable.

From 1600 to 1725, therefore, it was normal for the western powers to be engaged either in complicated manoeuvres to build up sympathetic political factions within the Baltic states or in long-drawn-out negotiations to secure commercial advantages. But on occasions they actually dominated the Baltic region, endeavouring to impose settlements in wars which interrupted trade and their schemes elsewhere. In the subsequent account of the struggle for power in the north it will be noted that time and again the strength of the English and Dutch fleets and the skill of French diplomacy were decisive; peace and a satisfactory balance of power in the Baltic were indispensable to the political and economic interests of the states of western Europe.

Further Reading

Charles E. Hill, *The Danish Sound Dues and the Command of the Baltic.* Duke University Press (Durham, North Carolina, 1926).

Robert Albion, *Forests and Sea Power.* Harvard University Press (Cambridge, Mass., 1926).

C. W. Cole, *Colbert and a Century of French Mercantilism.* Shoe String Press (Hamden, Conn., 1939).

G. Edmundson, *A History of Holland.* Cambridge University Press (Cambridge, 1922).

P. Geyl, *The Netherlands in the Seventeenth Century.* Benn (London: Part I, 1961; Part II, 1963).

Christopher Hill, *A Century of Revolution.* Nelson (London, 1961).

J. F. Chance, *George I and the Northern War*, Chapter 1. Smith, Elder (London, 1909).

G. N. Clark, *The Seventeenth Century.* Oxford University Press (paperback), (London, 1960).

J. F. Chance, 'England and Sweden in the Time of William III and Anne'. *English Historical Review*, Vol. XVI (1901).

Sea frozen for more than 3 months

The rest of Baltic Sea froze for a shorter period except in the
extreme west which was usually ice-free.
    Pack-ice was always a hazard in winter.

0   100   200   300   400 miles

PRODUCTS OF THE BALTIC IN THE SEVENTEENTH CENTURY

PART II
The Northern Powers
and the Baltic

The struggle of the northern states for power and influence over the Baltic reached its height in the seventeenth century. There seemed little doubt in the opening years that Denmark-Norway, with her command of the Sound, and her large navy, was the strongest power in the west, and that the huge expanse of Poland-Lithuania dominated the east. But in fact neither of these powers was able to maintain her position during the next hundred years. As the century advanced, Sweden rapidly extended her control, not only over the Baltic, but, for a time, over northern Europe. By the middle of the century, indeed, she appeared to have gained the much sought-after *dominium maris baltici*, in so far as this could be obtained by any Baltic state in the face of the commercial strength of the maritime powers of western Europe. But, at the close of the period, she encountered overwhelming opposition, not only from her old enemies, Denmark and Poland, but also from Prussia and Russia, two more dangerous foes. It is the remarkable story of Sweden's rise, and her equally dramatic decline, which is the central theme running through a study of the Baltic region in this century. What, then, were the motives and ambitions which lay behind the policies of the Baltic powers, and which culminated in the fierce conflict of the seventeenth century?

[7] DENMARK

In 1600 Denmark was much larger than it is today, with Copenhagen, its capital city, lying at the centre of a considerable
empire. Zealand, and the surrounding archipelago of over a
hundred islands, formed the heart of the state, with the provinces
of Skåne, Blekinge and Halland, culturally and economically
very important, lying across the Sound. Danish rule also extended
over the Jutland peninsula to Schleswig-Holstein, and out into
the Baltic Sea, where possession of the islands of Bornholm, Gotland and Ösel was of great strategic value. Above all, since 1380,
the kingdom of Norway had been ruled from Denmark. Thus it
was small wonder that Sweden sought to break out from what
amounted to encirclement by her neighbour.

This situation was not the result of an abundance of natural
resources in Denmark, as there was no mineral wealth and the
soil was generally poor. Moreover in contrast with the rest of
Scandinavia, Denmark was not a timber-producing land; her
exports were mainly agricultural, consisting of corn, cattle and
horses. Proximity to the sea resulted in seamanship and occupa-
tions connected with the sea being well-developed; thus fishing
was important and herring was caught in the Sound in considerable quantities. But Denmark, in the Middle Ages and early
modern times, could never have acquired so dominant a position,
had it not been for her tremendous geographical advantage
astride the Baltic Sea.

In the first place communications across the Sound to Norway,
which was economically very valuable to Denmark, were essential.
Certainly there was no doubt about the general poverty of
Norway's predominantly mountainous land, or the difficulty of
the peasants attempting to eke out a precarious existence, but
consolation was to be found in the abundance of fish, in particular
cod, herring and salmon, and in the vast resources of timber.
The demand for timber was rising constantly, and fish and such
products as cod-liver oil and blubber were much sought-after by
the countries bordering the southern Baltic and in the more

populous areas of Germany. It soon became clear that Norwegian trade was more important than Danish, and great efforts were made by the Danish monarchs to stimulate its growth. The loss of Halland across the Sound, in the middle of the seventeenth century, came as a great blow, for it was through this province that close communications between the two kingdoms were maintained.

But control of the channel between the Baltic and the North Seas was of even greater significance to the King of Denmark. According to Christian IV (King of Denmark 1596–1648), the Sound was the most brilliant jewel in his crown, and the rest of Europe fully understood the importance to Denmark of this maritime highway which also acted as a bridge between central and northern Europe. As the demand for Baltic products became greater, the kings of Denmark, by levying the famous 'Sound dues', exploited this geographical position to the utmost, with grave political consequences.

Danish kings found in the tolls they exacted from ships passing through the Sound and the Great Belt a steady source of income with which they were able to maintain a large navy and, when necessary, employ mercenary troops. These dues were levied as early as 1430, and were regarded as the private income of the Danish king until 1816 when they went to the public treasury. They were most unpopular with other nations and involved Denmark in many diplomatic and military struggles. Viggo Starcke, author of *Denmark in World History*,[1] has described them as a two-edged sword, pointing out that, although they brought in large sums of money, they resulted in considerable naval and military expenditure for their defence. He argues that it was Denmark's blockade policy in the Sound which resulted in conflicts with the maritime powers and the rest of Scandinavia, and which, in the long run, caused the loss of the eastern half of ancient Denmark. The actual business of levying the dues caused great delays in shipping and trade as there were elaborate regulations about rights of search in peace and war, requirements involving passports and the documentation of vessels and their

1. Philadelphia University Press (Philadelphia, 1963).

cargoes, all of which varied according to which nation was involved and its particular diplomatic relationship with Denmark. With the speeding up of modern trade and commerce these dues became increasingly irksome to the rest of the world; finally, in 1855, the United States of America stated that she would refuse to pay them after a period of twelve months. At an international conference the nations of the world agreed to pay Denmark the capitalized value of the dues and, in return, Denmark was to abolish the tolls and keep the Sound buoyed and lighted. Professor Charles E. Hill, in his valuable study, *The Danish Sound Dues and the Command of the Baltic*, argues convincingly that, although the King of Denmark relinquished a right which he had exercised for many years, that right was an 'anomaly in international relations and contrary to the customary regulation of straits'.

Indeed for centuries the kings of Denmark had regarded the Sound merely as a river flowing through their dominions. In 1445 the Danish royal residence was moved from Roskilde to Copenhagen on the coast, a city growing steadily in prosperity. By the middle of the sixteenth century the Sound dues were firmly established and, to emphasize Denmark's position, Frederick II built the great castle of Kronborg on the Sound. The Danish kings even considered it their right to levy tariffs on all ships trading with Russia, including those which sailed via the north of Norway to Archangel, thus avoiding the Sound dues. Consequently during this century the English company trading by this route paid an annual sum to Denmark for the privilege. The levying of tolls certainly played a major part in the hundred and fifty years of intermittent warfare between Denmark and Sweden; control of the Sound was seen by both sides as essential to any real command of the Baltic. In 1622 the Council of Christian IV assured him that supremacy of the Sound, and of the Baltic islands of Bornholm, Gotland and Ösel across as far as Courland, belonged by right to Denmark. They recognized the difficulty of maintaining Danish command of the sea between Ösel, Pernau and Riga, but suggested that this should be exercised according to opportunity. The rapid increase in the power of Sweden in the early seventeenth century, particularly when Gustavus Adolphus obtained the right to levy dues along the commercially rich stretch of Prussian coast, was regarded as a serious threat. In 1638, a pamphlet, *Mare Clausum*, by an anonymous author, was published by Christian IV. It argued that the King of Denmark was supreme over the Baltic and that this was attested by many incidents in the past as well as by the fact that he owned the Sound and the Belts, the keys to the Baltic. None the less, during the seventeenth century, the Danes were unable either to end Sweden's long-established exemption from the Sound dues or to prevent her from conquering the north coast of the Sound itself. Denmark was thus forced to give up the claim to supremacy and from 1660 she bent all her energies on revenge and the recovery of her lost provinces.

[8] SWEDEN

In the Middle Ages Sweden had lagged far behind her more populous and wealthy neighbour, and had had to take second place in the Kalmar Union, 1397–1523, formed by Queen Margaret of Norway, during which Norway, Denmark and Sweden were united under one sovereign. This project was, however, too vast and Margaret's successors made many serious errors. An absentee government left the control of Sweden in the hands of the hated Crown Bailiffs and this resulted in a strong national reaction. It culminated in the destruction of the Union and the establishment of the Vasa dynasty in Sweden in the person of Gustavus Vasa (1523–60).

Gustavus Vasa was soon struggling against what must have seemed overwhelming odds, not least of which was the geographical weakness of Sweden. The southern coasts, bordering the Sound, were in the hands of Denmark, and Sweden only possessed a narrow strip of land, about eleven miles wide, as an ice-free outlet to the North Sea. This strip of land at the mouth of the river Göta Älv ran between the Norwegian province of Bohuslän and the Danish province of Halland and, to defend their trade, in particular their vital salt supplies, in such a precarious position, the Swedes built the fortress of Älvsborg. This stronghold was coveted by the Danes, and temporarily captured more than once; permanent seizure would make Sweden economically and politically dependent on the Sound for all communication with the west. Thus from the point of view of trade and defence Sweden was extremely vulnerable. In addition Denmark's possession of the island of Gotland was a danger to the security of eastern Sweden (including Stockholm), to the maintenance of communications with Finland (part of Sweden since the fourteenth century), and to Swedish trade with the German Baltic coastlands in the south. In the east, the rising power of Muscovy was a threat to Finland itself and to the territories on the southern coast of the Gulf of Finland, ruled with ever-increasing helplessness by the Teutonic Knights. Sweden soon clashed with both Russia and Poland over these provinces and Denmark also staked her claim. The Seven Years' War of the North, 1563–70, between Denmark and Sweden, was largely the result of Denmark's ambitions in the eastern Baltic where she intended to complete her chain of strategic bases from the Sound to the Gulf of Finland, and incidentally hem in Sweden completely. Thus the latter's primary aim must be to strengthen her geographical position: in doing so she found herself in fierce conflict with Denmark and, eventually, with all the Baltic powers.

Economically, also, Sweden was far less advanced than Denmark although she was potentially richer in natural resources. The most fertile areas lay around Lake Mälaren, in the provinces of Västergothland and Östergothland and along the coastal plain of Finland. But elsewhere the soil was poor and the thinly-scattered communities just managed to exist on their own produce. Central Sweden, often referred to as the Bergslagen area from the special privileges granted to it in the Middle Ages, had been known since the thirteenth century to be rich in minerals. But it was not until the seventeenth century that the real value of these resources was seen when Swedish trade in these commodities with western Europe developed rapidly. The same situation existed with regard to Sweden's great expanses of forest which were soon to yield quantities of timber, tar and pitch for export, and charcoal for the developing iron industry. Finland was also a rich source of timber and was particularly important for the manufacture of tar, while at the head of the Gulf of Bothnia the fur trade was expanding steadily. Gustavus Vasa founded Helsingfors with which he hoped to rival the trading centres on the opposite shore of the Gulf of Finland in Estonia and Livonia, and the capture of these two provinces later was to be of the utmost importance in expanding the valuable trade with Russia which had been developing since the thirteenth century. Clearly Sweden's growth depended on exploiting her natural resources and building up her commerce both inside the Baltic and with the rest of Europe. The possibilities in these fields were well understood by the German traders of the Hanseatic League who had succeeded in dominating Sweden's trade for a long period. In particular the development of the Swedish mining industries was the result of the enterprise of German financiers and mining experts. Lübeck and other cities were granted enormous advantages in Swedish trade in return for their help in the war of independence against Denmark, and Gustavus Vasa's first great task was to break their monopoly. Once this was done Sweden made rapid commercial strides until, little more than a hundred years later, Axel Oxenstierna (Chancellor of Gustavus Adolphus) was able to speak of controlling all the important ports in the Baltic and thus regulating the flow of corn and naval stores to the rest of Europe.

The newly-established Vasa monarchy made important progress in strengthening Sweden's economic and political position in the Baltic. The reign of Gustavus Vasa was significant for internal consolidation and, in particular, for Sweden's break with the Church of Rome and her adoption of the Lutheran faith which was destined to have far-reaching consequences upon later foreign policy. Moreover in 1525, Danish and Swedish forces, in temporary cooperation, defeated Lübeck which was supporting the dethroned Christian II of Denmark and, as a result, Sweden was freed from Lübeck's economic domination. Among other achievements, Gustavus Vasa strengthened the finances of the state, reorganized the mines, improved the army and developed the navy with large ships of modern design. Above all, he secured the succession to the throne in the dynasty of the House of Vasa. Gustavus Adolphus commented of his grandfather: 'This King Gustavus was the instrument by which God again raised up our fatherland to prosperity'.

On the whole this progress was maintained although neither of Gustavus Vasa's immediate successors, his sons Eric XIV, 1560–8, and John III, 1568–92, were of the same calibre as their father, and their policies revealed a lack of stability. Conflict with Denmark resulted from Eric's policy of expansion in Estonia and, during the Seven Years' War of the North, the Swedish navy, further improved by Eric XIV, was a match for the Danish fleet. But the ransom demanded for the return of Älvsborg, conquered by the Danes, was a heavy sacrifice, and forcibly brought home Swedish insecurity in the west. John III continued the policy of expansion in the eastern Baltic in the hope of controlling Russian trade, and, in 1581, Estonia and Narva fell into Swedish hands. By this date, indeed, Sweden's influence in Baltic politics could no longer be ignored.

John III had married a Roman Catholic Polish Princess and, in 1587, his son was elected to the Polish throne as Sigismund III. Despite this the two countries were unable to work in harmony. Their interests clashed violently in Livonia, and when Sigismund succeeded to the Swedish throne on the death of his father in 1592 he became involved in a major constitutional and religious crisis. Brought up a Roman Catholic, married into the House of Habsburg, he was seen by Rome, and indeed saw himself, as reconquering Sweden for the Catholic faith. Moreover this was at a time when Spain and the Empire were toying with the possibility of extending their influence into the Baltic. Eventually, in 1599, the Swedes deposed Sigismund, and his uncle, the third son of Gustavus Vasa, became Regent, and later accepted the Crown as Charles IX. Poland and Sweden remained open enemies for more than fifty years, and Charles IX, and later his son, Gustavus Adolphus, attempted to represent Sigismund in the eyes of Europe as embodying the threat of the Counter-

Reformation to the Protestant north. Thus Sweden became involved in the much wider European struggle culminating in the Thirty Years' War.

At the accession of Gustavus Adolphus in 1611 an uneasy armistice existed between Sweden and Poland, but the latter's growing influence in Russia during the 'Time of Troubles', and the apparent possibility of a Polish czar, were increasing the likelihood of war in the eastern Baltic. Also the conflict with Russia over Ingria and Estonia was unresolved and Sweden was again drifting into war with Denmark; there were long-standing differences concerning the Scandinavian Arctic coastlands, problems over the Sound dues, and friction resulting from Sweden's blockade of the rich Livonian port of Riga. By 1611 hostilities had begun and Sweden, internally weak, was in no state to conduct a war for supremacy of the Baltic. She had indeed made considerable advances over the last ninety years, and internationally she was in a far stronger position than she had been after her war of independence. Nevertheless there seemed a very real danger that Denmark would become once and for all the master of the Baltic, that Sweden would be cut off from her trade with Russia and that she would lose her vital outlet in the west. In short her very existence was at stake. The transformation which subsequently took place in the balance of power in the western Baltic, substituting Swedish for Danish dominance, is among the most remarkable episodes in modern European history. Likewise in the eastern Baltic, the ambitions of Poland and Muscovy were doomed to be shattered by the sudden growth of Swedish power.

During the sixteenth century the prestige and influence of Poland had been at its height. This state had originated in the land between the rivers Oder and Vistula about the tenth century but, with the movement eastward of the Germanic tribes, its centre became stabilized mainly around the Vistula and its tributaries. The boundary in the south was the ridge of the Carpathian mountains, but elsewhere the lack of clear natural frontiers became, later, a serious threat to Poland's existence. (In the eighteenth century Poland disappeared from the map altogether, wiped out by her greedy neighbours, Russia, Prussia and Austria.) A dynastic alliance had been formed in the fourteenth century with Lithuania which bordered Poland in the north-east, and by 1569 the two states were definitely joined. They had been brought together by the common danger in the north from the Teutonic Knights who controlled the south coast of the Gulf of Finland. After a prolonged struggle with the Knights of Prussia during the fifteenth century, Poland gained her natural outlet, the mouth of the Vistula, upon which stood the great port of Danzig, the centre of the timber and corn trade both of Poland and of the eastern Baltic in general. From the east, centre and north of Poland came quantities of fir, while oak was transported from as far south as Galicia. The great corn-producing plains of Poland were dependent on Danzig for their trade with the west, and the importance of this strip of Prussian coastline to a country with difficult access to the sea was generally realized.

During the following century Poland's long struggle began with the growing state of Muscovy; Ivan the Terrible in vain waged a war which lasted for a quarter of a century (1558–83) to gain possession of Livonia. The King of Poland feared that once Moscow obtained an enlarged outlet to the Baltic and constructed a fleet, all free commerce and shipping in the area would be at an end. In 1578, King Stephen Batory argued before the Polish Diet that Ivan wished to use Livonia as a base for further advances in East Prussia and Lithuania, and thus eventually to control the

Baltic. For the time, however, Muscovy failed. Poland was still the stronger power, having made considerable gains at Russia's expense around Kiev and Smolensk. Furthermore as a result of the extinction of Ivan the Terrible's line, Russia sank into the 'Time of Troubles', 1604–13, and Poland took full advantage of the situation. Moscow itself was actually conquered twice, and Sigismund III installed, temporarily, his son and heir as czar. Indeed Poland seemed on the point of destroying her neighbour and extending her territory along the Baltic coast to the north and east, taking in Livonia once and for all. At Danzig Sigismund was energetically constructing a Polish navy which was soon able to inflict damage on Baltic trade, and in 1627, it actually defeated an unprepared Swedish squadron.

As the seventeenth century progressed this situation rapidly changed. Poland, beset with internal difficulties, was unable to prevent Sweden, already the master of Estonia, from extending her power over Livonia and, for a time, over the whole of the eastern Baltic. Nor was she able to destroy the power of the Elector of Brandenburg in East Prussia. Quite against her will, Poland was forced to extend the power of the Hohenzollern electors over this territory, and it was they who, in the eighteenth century, first cut Poland's vital artery to the Baltic by acquiring West Prussia. But, in the long run, the state to gain most power in this region was Poland's old enemy, Russia. The increasingly disorganized Poles gradually lost more and more territory, including Kiev and Smolensk and, by the middle of the century, the relationship between the two Slav powers was completely reversed, with Poland clearly the weaker. Ultimately, exhausted by long wars with Turkey, she could do nothing to prevent Russia opening her 'window on the west', thus, at last, regaining an outlet to the Baltic.

Russia's 'urge to the sea' in the north-western corner of her empire was many centuries old, and had brought her into conflict with Swedes, Germans and Poles. Between the thirteenth and the fifteenth centuries, the Russian city of Novgorod was the centre of thriving trade with the west, largely conducted by the Hanse merchants. The most valuable exports were furs, including squirrel, sable, marten, fox and beaver. Fishing, sealing and whaling were important, as was the timber industry, and such commodities as flax, hemp, tar and pitch. This valuable and ever-increasing trade was looked upon with envy by the rising power of Moscow in the region of the Volga river, and attempts were frequently made to conquer Novgorod. In the fifteenth century this aim was achieved, but the subsequent shutting out of the Hanse merchants from the city meant that they transferred their activities to towns on the coast of the Gulf of Finland, such as Reval and Narva and, above all, Riga in Livonia. The importance of these towns as Russian trade routes was fully understood not only by the Muscovites, but also by the Poles and the Swedes. Thus during the sixteenth century Muscovy in vain sought to extend her power along the Baltic coast, only to see Livonia fall into Polish hands, at least for the time, and to see Estonia and Narva go to Sweden. The latter's obvious defence of her positions in Finland and Estonia was the conquest of all the territory around the head of the Gulf of Finland, thus excluding Russia altogether from access to the Baltic. In particular the Swedes desired two strategic points, the river Neva which connected the Gulf of Finland with lake Ladoga, and the river Volkhov, upon which stood Novgorod, and which connected lake Ladoga with lake Ilmen (see map). Sweden, like Poland, seized her opportunity during Russia's 'Time of Troubles', and in 1617, at the Peace of Stolbovo, she gained all she wished except Novgorod which was in any case cut off from all access to the Baltic. Gustavus Adolphus was quick to see the advantages for Sweden. In January 1617, in a speech to the Riksdag (Parliament), he stated:

Thus our position has made things more difficult for the Russians, in this, that they have been cut off from the shores of the Baltic. Henceforth they are forbidden entrance to the Baltic at any point, and cannot use it for their ships for their own accommodation, either for war purposes or for trade, without our special permission.[2]

Again, in August, after the Peace of Stolbovo, Gustavus Adolphus emphasized the economic value to Sweden of a land in which

There are rivers and lakes with a wealth of fish. Wherever there are forests, they have become large and dense during these many years of unrest, and are filled with all kinds of game, the pelts of which are very valuable. If God grants us an extension of the peace, this country with all its strange resources will greatly increase Sweden's revenue. I shall refrain from mentioning at this point the large sums of money a modest and uniform duty may bring, because the trade of all Russia has to go through these countries.

Looking back it is obvious that Russia would endeavour to break out from this position as soon as possible, and recover the strategic points in the hands of Sweden. But Russia was for many years very weak, and her isolation made it more difficult for her to obtain the knowledge and the skills of western Europe which she needed to strengthen her position. It was not until the end of our period that the Baltic outlet was finally recovered and Peter the Great had achieved his goal. But from that time onwards, the rapid growth of trade between western Europe and Russia, and the latter's increasing power and influence in European politics, bore witness to her need of free access to the sea, a need more vital to Russia than to any other Baltic power.

2. Quoted by Robert J. Kerner, *The Urge to the Sea: The Course of Russian History*, California University Press (Berkeley, 1942).

[11] BRANDENBURG-PRUSSIA

During the seventeenth century Brandenburg-Prussia revealed unexpected Baltic ambitions. The Electorate of Brandenburg was situated in the north-eastern part of the German Empire, on land originally conquered from the Slavs. At the opening of the seventeenth century it was obscure, with no outlet to the sea, few resources and a poor sandy soil. Its inhabitants were sparsely scattered and even one hundred years later the population per square mile was smaller than in practically any other area of Germany. That Brandenburg should have become at times a serious threat to Sweden, the strongest seventeenth century Baltic power, must have been extremely difficult for contemporaries to understand or accept.

As early as the beginning of the sixteenth century the ruler of Brandenburg had revealed designs on the Baltic coastline. He suggested to the Emperor that he should expel the Danes from Germany in return for the duchy of Holstein, an offer which was refused. But the seventeenth century had not run many years before the Hohenzollern family, the rulers of Brandenburg, acquired the Baltic duchy of East Prussia. It was geographically in a much better situation than Brandenburg, and was more prosperous. Its most important town, Königsberg, was a thriving commercial centre in the eastern Baltic, its trade based on the export of corn, hemp, flax and other products from Poland and eastern Europe and the import of cloth and manufactured goods from western Europe. Over a hundred years earlier, a member of the younger branch of the Hohenzollern family had been elected as the Grand Master of the Order of Teutonic Knights which governed the duchy and, during the following years, the Elector of Brandenburg obtained the right to the succession in East Prussia from its overlord, the King of Poland. In 1605, the Elector was permitted to administer the duchy on behalf of the insane Prince Albert Frederick, the last of the younger branch of the family and, in 1618, when Prince Albert died, the Elector John Sigismund, in return for a subsidy to Poland for the Turkish war, was allowed to remain as the ruler of East Prussia. Fifty years later the Great Elector (1640–88), with great cunning, extorted the recognition of his full sovereignty over the territory from both Sweden and Poland. There now remained West or Polish Prussia, the vital artery of Poland, lying between the two main possessions of the Hohenzollerns; it was clear to Charles XII of Sweden, during his extensive campaigns in Poland at the turn of the century, that Brandenburg-Prussia would take the first reasonable opportunity to seize this region, thus securing not only the communications between Brandenburg and East Prussia, but also the important trading centre of Danzig. But, as it turned out, Brandenburg-Prussia was to be denied geographical unity for almost another century.

East Prussia was not the only land acquired on the Baltic coast by Brandenburg in the seventeenth century. In 1648, at the Peace of Westphalia, the Great Elector received the duchy of Eastern Pomerania, of whose duke he was acknowledged heir. In fact the whole of Pomerania, with its long stretch of coastline and its good ports, was looked upon by Brandenburg as essential to her economic and political expansion. But, in 1648, the territory was divided between Brandenburg and Sweden, and the former failed to acquire the important port of Stettin at the mouth of the river Oder. From this time, Stettin was the object of Brandenburg's ambition, for, despite the very real gains made along the Baltic coast, the state still had no really good harbour. In 1677 Stettin was actually conquered from Sweden although it had to be restored when peace was made two years later. It was not until the general dismemberment of Sweden, at the Peace of Nystad in 1721, that Prussia finally achieved her aim. Nevertheless, in order to increase the trade of Brandenburg and reduce the importance of Stettin, the Great Elector had built a canal, completed in the 1660s, to link the rivers Oder and Spree (a tributary of the river Elbe), by which he successfully diverted traffic via his capital city, Berlin, through the canal to the Elbe, and thus away from the mouth of the Oder. As a result, Berlin, hitherto a very insignificant city, grew steadily, while Stettin and Frankfurt-on-Oder declined.

It was the Great Elector who first sought to establish a Prussian naval force on the Baltic Sea. About ten ships were brought together by a Dutch merchant on behalf of the Elector in the early 1670s. The new fleet remained small but it saw some action during the following war against Sweden. On the Great Elector's death in 1688 it disappeared, but its very existence was a new phenomenon in Baltic politics and a significant pointer to the future.

When a careful look is taken at the political and economic aspirations of the Baltic powers in the seventeenth century it is impossible not to agree with Professor Michael Roberts in his comment that 'The ambitions of the Baltic powers must probably in any case come into violent conflict'.[3] With the decline of the Hanseatic League from commercial supremacy, and with the collapse in the east of the political power of the Teutonic Knights, a crisis had been reached in the history of the northern states.

3. Michael Roberts, *Gustavus Adolphus: A History of Sweden*, 1611-1632, 2 vols., Longmans (London, 1953).

Further Reading

General

Relevant volumes of the *Cambridge Modern History* and the *New Cambridge Modern History*.

R. NISBET BAIN, *Scandinavia*. Cambridge University Press (Cambridge, 1905).
S. M. TOYNE, *The Scandinavians in History*. Arnold (London, 1948).
D. MALAND, *Europe in the Seventeenth Century*. Macmillan (London, 1966).
W. F. REDDAWAY, *Select Documents of European History*, Vol. II, 1492–1715. Methuen (London, 1930).

Sweden
C. HALLENDORFF and A. SCHÜCK, *A History of Sweden*. Cassell (London, 1929).

INGVAR ANDERSSON, *A History of Sweden*. Weidenfeld (London, 1955).

S. OAKLEY, *The Story of Sweden*. Faber (London, 1966).

MICHAEL ROBERTS, *Essays in Swedish History*. Weidenfeld and Nicolson (London, 1967).

MICHAEL ROBERTS (ed.), *Sweden as a Great Power 1611–1697*. 'Documents of Modern History'. Edward Arnold (London, 1968).

E. JUTIKKALA, *A History of Finland*. Thames & Hudson (London, 1962).

Denmark

J. H. S. BIRCH, *Denmark in History*. Murray (London, 1938).

T. K. DERRY, *A Short History of Norway*. Allen & Unwin (London, 1957).

Poland

W. F. REDDAWAY (ed.), *The Cambridge History of Poland*, 2 vols. Cambridge University Press (Cambridge, 1951).

OSCAR HALECKI, *A History of Poland*. Dent (London, 1961).

Russia

B. H. SUMNER, *A Survey of Russian History*. Duckworth (London, 1944).

R. CHARQUES, *A Short History of Russia*. Phoenix (London, 1956).

J. LAWRENCE, *Russia in the Making*. Allen & Unwin (London, 1957).

B. PARES, *A History of Russia*. Cape (London, 1962).

Prussia

F. L. CARSTEN, *The Origins of Prussia*. Clarendon Press (Oxford, 1954).

S. FAY, *The Rise of Brandenburg-Prussia to 1786*. 'Berkshire Studies in European History'. Holt, Rinehart & Winston (New York and London, 1964).

R. FLENLEY, *Modern German History*. Dent (London, 1964).

Part II

CHARLES E. HILL, *Danish Sound Dues and the Command of the Baltic*. Duke University Press (Durham, N. Carolina, 1926).

ROBERT J. KERNER, *The Urge to the Sea: The Course of Russian History*. California University Press (Berkeley, 1942).

MICHAEL ROBERTS, *The Early Vasas: a History of Sweden 1523–1611*. Cambridge University Press (Cambridge, 1968).

PART III
Sweden—A Great Power

The history of Sweden during the period 1611–48 is truly remarkable. This state, in such a critical position both at home and
abroad when Gustavus Adolphus succeeded to the throne, on the
verge of bankruptcy and apparently about to succumb to its
three great rivals, Denmark, Poland and Russia, in twenty years
became the strongest military power in Europe and changed the
course of history. Denmark had been humbled, valuable territory
seized from Poland and Russia, the Habsburg forces defeated,
and, in alliance with France, Sweden had imposed her will on
Germany and was acknowledged as the leader of Protestant
Europe. Simultaneously her internal condition was transformed
to an astonishing degree by a whole series of creative reforms.
Indeed Sweden's progress during these years can be compared
with the rise of Brandenburg-Prussia as one of the miracles of
modern history. How was it that this hitherto almost unnoticed
country became involved to such a degree in the mainstream of
European affairs, and how could Sweden sustain such a mighty
effort?

Not least among the factors which account for this is the
weakness of Sweden's neighbours in Europe during this period.
Nations which later challenged and ultimately overwhelmed
Sweden were at this time in no position to compete with her.
But this in itself does not provide an adequate explanation. The
real answer lies in the sheer creative genius of Gustavus Adolphus,
King of Sweden 1611–32, who worked with his chancellor, Axel
Oxenstierna.

In every direction, in every sphere, whether civil or military, domestic or foreign, the King and his minister initiated reforms and made constructive plans. Certainly Sweden's rivals were, in various ways, temporarily weaker, but monarchs such as the able and courageous Christian IV of Denmark had the misfortune to rule at the same time as a man who may be considered not merely as Sweden's greatest king, but as one of the greatest monarchs in history.

His life-long, loyal partner, Oxenstierna, was a genius of a different sort, with a first-class aptitude for administration and diplomacy and with high political courage. The history of Sweden during this period is their joint work, the product of a formidable partnership.

[12] SWEDEN'S PROBLEMS IN 1611

The death of Charles IX faced his seventeen-year-old son with an accumulation of formidable difficulties, the most pressing of which was an imminent constitutional crisis. Gustavus Adolphus's succession was the signal for an attempt to clarify the complicated relations which had developed between the King, the Nobles and the Estates. During the sixteenth century, the medieval Council of the Realm, or *Riksrad*, composed of the great nobles, had lost its former power, partly as a result of troubles over independence, and partly because of the prestige of the new Vasa dynasty and the economic strength which the Crown derived from the Reformation. Government was still personal and the Vasas relied not on the aristocracy but on low-born secretaries to carry out their wishes. During the century, as the business of government grew, the administration became inefficient and too complex for one man to control. Thus in the latter part of the sixteenth century demands increased from a new generation of nobles led by Eric Sparre, that the King should restore them to their rightful place in affairs. In particular they objected to the way the king used a comparatively new body, the

Diet, or *Riksdag*, to achieve his ends. The accession to the Swedish throne in 1592 of Sigismund III, King of Poland, complicated matters further. Eventually the nobles threw in their lot with Sigismund in opposition to Duke Charles who relied on the Riksdag. In 1599 the latter deposed Sigismund, and Charles, who took over the government, dealt harshly with the aristocracy. He relied again on secretaries and for the rest of his reign ruled amid an atmosphere of intrigue and suspicion. Thus in 1611 the nobles were determined that Gustavus Adolphus should not govern as his father had done and, in the Charter of 1612, which they forced the King to accept before they would recognize his title, it seemed they had triumphed. Gustavus Adolphus promised to give all the great offices of state to the nobles and make no new laws, or declare war or peace without their consent. Furthermore he agreed not to summon the Riksdag too often. It remained to be seen whether this would seriously curtail the power of the King, whether harmony would prevail, or, indeed, whether Gustavus Adolphus would, like his father, attempt to ignore all opposition.

But the resolving of the constitutional issue, at least for the time, certainly did not ensure security for Gustavus Adolphus. Apart from the fact that Sweden was engaged in war with both Denmark and Russia, Sigismund III of Poland had by no means abandoned his claim to the throne and his agents were at work everywhere disseminating his propaganda. In 1600 there were about four hundred Swedish exiles living in Poland, all anxious for revenge on Charles IX and his son. Thus Gustavus Adolphus was constantly threatened by rumours and plots and with the prospect of a Polish invasion. His accession in 1611 presented an extremely favourable opportunity to Sigismund and the danger from Poland was at its height during the next few years. But fortunately the Polish king was busy pursuing his schemes in Russia and had his own internal troubles.

To these external threats must be added the feeble, unpopular administration in Sweden. Lawlessness and anarchy prevailed, the armed forces were poorly trained and disciplined, and the country hovered on the verge of bankruptcy. This situation was made worse by the enormous ransom imposed at the Peace of Knäred in 1613 for the vital port of Älvsborg which the Danes had captured the year before, thus cutting Sweden off from the Atlantic and seriously threatening the growing trade in salt and minerals with the maritime powers. Finally any reforming activity by the government was impeded by the large tracts of land which had been made over to members of the royal family who ruled them practically independently of the Crown. It was indeed fortunate for Sweden that the son of Charles IX was a man of no ordinary talents.

[13] GUSTAVUS ADOLPHUS (1611–32) AND OXENSTIERNA

Gustavus Adolphus was carefully educated and prepared for his future tasks both by his father and an excellent tutor, John Skytte. The latter was learned and had travelled widely, and his pupil was given a good academic training. Gustavus Adolphus showed early promise; in particular he revealed an aptitude for languages, an interest in mathematics and mechanics, and an understanding of the theory and technicalities of warfare. He had inherited the Vasa gift for vivid oratory and was initiated early by his father into the practical side of kingship. He attended Council meetings from the age of ten and before his accession had visited many different parts of the lands he was to inherit. His personality developed rapidly and he was fully able to take over the government while still technically a minor. He soon revealed a strong sense of duty and service, the ability to choose able and reliable subordinates and to inspire them to do their utmost. His political talents, his gift for leadership, his piety and charm, his originality and far-sightedness, qualified him indeed to be hailed as the greatest of Swedish kings. Moreover he found a statesman of first rank in Axel Oxenstierna, the leader of the nobles. The Chancellor was a man of different temperament, but his calmness,

experience and judgment, complemented the more fiery qualities
of his master, who fully appreciated Oxenstierna's great courage
and devotion. In twenty years there were no open quarrels
between them and there is little evidence that they differed on
fundamental policy. They were firm friends and treated each
other with frankness and respect. Together they bent their
energies first to tackling the problems threatening Sweden with
collapse, and then, with conspicuous success, to reconstructing
the whole fabric of the state.

Fears of another reign of constitutional tension were soon dis-
pelled. Gustavus had appointed the leader of the Riksrad (Oxenstierna) as his Chancellor and henceforth abided loyally by his
promise of 1612, giving the high offices of state to the nobles. In
fact his succession inaugurated a period of collaboration between
the Crown and the aristocracy. They soon found that they could
trust the King not to abuse his position and when, on occasions,
he found it necessary to violate the Charter they remained un-
moved. Gustavus Adolphus became truly the leader of the nation;
his government was strong and popular. He took full advantage
of the military talents and administrative ability to be found
among the nobility, and he thus succeeded in solving the problem
of royal authority versus noble ambition. Whether this situation
would last under monarchs of a different calibre was another
matter.

[14] REFORM IN SWEDEN

The administration

It was in partnership with the nobility that Gustavus Adolphus
and Oxenstierna carried out their reconstruction of the administration, a reconstruction without which Sweden could never have
achieved her position of power in Europe. The primitive, peri-
patetic government of 1611 would have been quite useless in

later years when the King and his chief minister were abroad for long periods, dependent on vast sums of money and a constant flow of military supplies and men collected and dispatched from Sweden. The new government machine centred around the five existing officers of state, the High Steward, Marshal, Admiral, Chancellor and Treasurer, and the beginning really came in 1614 when the Judicature Ordinance set up a Supreme Court under the High Steward. It was situated in Stockholm and, in theory at least, its procedure and methods were fully organized. In 1618 the Exchequer Ordinance set up a Collegium (or Board), consisting of the Treasurer and five Councillors, in an attempt to clarify national finances. The Chancery soon underwent the same treatment, and ably directed by Oxenstierna, this office, at the very nerve-centre of events, brought about increased efficiency in many spheres of government. The War Office and the Admiralty did not fully develop this structure until 1634 but the direction had been clearly indicated in the preceding years. The heads of all the departments were situated in Stockholm which henceforth developed into a true capital city, and the body of nobles, frequently left to carry on the government, found their burden of duties increasingly heavy.

The most significant point in this reform of the administration is that the King did not have to be present for his government to be carried on efficiently and this principle comes out strongly in the Form of Government of 1634. As a result, this document, drafted by Oxenstierna after the death of Gustavus Adolphus, has been regarded by some, including Christina and Charles X, as anti-monarchical, designed to give Oxenstierna more power, and representing the triumph of the nobility. In reality there is little justification for this. The Form of Government fits in with, and rounds off, the scheme of administrative reorganization which had been devised during Gustavus's reign, and it is very probable that he would have approved. None the less these government reforms were in the main the work of Oxenstierna, and the King did not always agree. Naturally the task was not completed at once, nor did the new departments always work smoothly, but the system gradually clarified until by 1634 Sweden was equipped with the most modern administrative system in Europe. Professor Michael Roberts comments on the importance of these reforms to the subsequent military success of Sweden:

Without the Exchequer Ordinance, the Judicature Ordinance, the Chancery Ordinance, Stralsund could hardly have been held, nor Breitenfeld won.[1]

Simultaneously local government came under the scrutiny of the King and his minister, for it was realized that any real mobilization of the resources of the state depended on an efficient provincial administration. The Swedish lands were divided clearly into twenty-three administrative districts. Each district, or *län*, was governed by a representative of the Crown and he dealt with the business of his *län* in much the same way as the King in his kingdom. He was aided by an efficient staff and governed according to Instructions drawn up by the King in 1624 and later supplemented in 1635. The reforms set on foot in this sphere were among the most important achievements of the reign.

These years, moreover, saw a development in the position of the Riksdag (or National Assembly). By 1632 it was established as part of the regular government machinery, its legislation recognized as valid, and its consent necessary for any new taxation or other burdens. In 1617 the Riksdag Ordinance had laid down the number of estates as four – the nobility, the clergy, the burghers and the peasants – and regulated procedure. The most important estate, the nobility, was itself placed on a more methodical basis in 1626, and qualifications for entry into the estate clearly defined. With regard to the estate of peasants (representing the Crown and freehold peasantry), it should be noted that this body had greater rights in the constitution than did any similar social group elsewhere in Europe. But the Riksdag certainly did not initiate legislation and was not by any means the sole legislative power. It was not yet a Parliament and was many decades behind its contemporary assembly in England.

1. Michael Roberts, op. cit.

Economic affairs

The ultimate strength of the nation depended on sound economic foundations. This was fully realized by Gustavus Adolphus who exerted all his energies to remedy the chaotic situation in which Sweden found herself in 1611. He made some mistakes, took unsound decisions, and in fact never really succeeded in mastering this side of affairs. But when this is said, the transformation brought about by the end of the reign is very striking, and without this progress, Sweden could never have developed into a dynamic military power.

In desperate need of ready money, the Crown, in the sixteenth century, had resorted to making over many of its sources of income to private persons as rewards, in discharge of debts, or in return for loans. Gustavus Adolphus continued this policy throughout his reign with serious repercussions later. But this by no means solved the financial problem, neither did internal taxation, even though this was kept at the highest possible level. On top of this came the enormous indemnity for Älvsborg which Christian IV was convinced Sweden could not pay, and which indeed was only discharged with great suffering. In the end it was really paid in copper exports which were in great demand, particularly in the Netherlands, but as a result Sweden was still heavily indebted to the Dutch at the end of Gustavus Adolphus's reign. The dearth of cash even at the best of times resulted from Sweden's continuing dependence on a natural economy, and when the nation became organized for war on a grand scale it was quite clear to the King and his Chancellor that neither ordinary nor extraordinary taxation would meet the extreme demands for vast sums of money, often required at short notice. But Sweden did finance her wars, and she did so because her leaders took advantage of the enormous opportunities to be found in the exploitation of the customs duties on Swedish Baltic ports, in the development of Sweden's mineral resources (in particular copper), and in making war pay for itself by placing the main burden not on Sweden but on Germany. Indeed Professor Roberts[2] argues convincingly that, provided these conditions

2. Michael Roberts, op. cit.

prevailed, Sweden's resources were not unduly strained, and that it was only after the Thirty Years' War, when the Prussian tolls were lost, copper was less in demand, and the mercenary markets of Germany declined, that it is true to say that Sweden could not in the long run maintain her position in Europe.

The largest single source of steady income was obtained from the tolls levied by Sweden after 1626 along the valuable stretch of Prussian coast which took in many rich Baltic ports. This customs barrier, which hampered neutral shipping and which extended along the Gulf of Finland as far as the river Neva, was most efficiently administered by Oxenstierna who levied the tolls at extortionate rates and also extracted heavy harbour dues. The loss of the Prussian duties was keenly felt in 1635 when the twenty-six-year truce was signed with Poland.

But there was a time when even the tolls were overshadowed by Swedish copper exports, energetically encouraged by the government. Sweden's mineral potentialities had been first revealed during the sixteenth century and foreign capital and skilled labour were already flowing into the country; the fine-quality iron from Swedish mines won world-wide acclaim, and copper, though growing in importance, remained the secondary metal. But gradually the great copper mines at Falun began to react to increasing foreign demand until, by the middle of Gustavus Adolphus's reign copper occupied a position of supreme importance in the economic life of the country. Foreign capital and skilled labour were offered every inducement to come to Sweden, while at the same time, many of Sweden's potential competitors in the copper market were ruined by the troubles in Germany. In 1630 Oxenstierna wrote:

Copper is the noblest commodity that the Swedish Crown produces and can boast of, wherein also a great part of the Crown's welfare stands; and therefore it is most reasonable that we address ourselves to exploit that mine, and to raise and maintain the price of copper, so that the might and riches of our country, and the revenues of the Crown, may be strengthened and increased.[3]

3. *Rikslanseren Axel Oxenstiernas Skrifter och brelvaxling*, I, i, 344. Quoted by Michael Roberts, op. cit.

The history of Gustavus Adolphus's attempts to stimulate a
somewhat declining demand for copper in Europe and his endeavours to persuade foreigners to adopt a copper coinage is somewhat unfortunate, but these difficulties and mistakes do not alter
the plain economic fact that during this period Swedish copper
monopolized the European market and provided Gustavus
Adolphus with large sums of money.

Progress was made likewise in the iron industry; new techniques were introduced and foreign capital attracted. The production of munitions and manufactured goods expanded rapidly and
by 1632, not only was iron-ore one of Sweden's main sources of
wealth, but the industry was capable of satisfying most of the
demands made on it for armaments by Sweden's enormous military forces in Germany. In Louis de Geer, a Dutchman, Gustavus Adolphus found a man of remarkable ability and great
wealth who took charge of the armaments industry and who
stimulated numerous other industrial enterprises such as brass,
tin, salt-petre and shipbuilding, to the great benefit of his
adopted country. (In 1644 he astounded Europe by fitting out
thirty ships at his own expense to fight against Denmark.)

As Sweden's export trade in these commodities increased,
Gustavus Adolphus, appreciating the importance of a flourishing
trade to the welfare of the nation, endeavoured to develop a
strong mercantile marine and to encourage Swedish merchants to
shake off the long-established hold on their commerce of the
Germans and the Dutch. The growth of Göteborg on the west
coast, after 1619, illustrates clearly that Sweden's trade was no
longer confined mainly to the German Baltic coast, and that her
commercial enterprises were expanding rapidly. There is little
doubt that Sweden's greatness depended at the bottom on her
industrial and commercial development during these years.

The army

But administrative reorganization and economic expansion were
not in themselves enough. Sweden's power in Europe was based
on armed strength and it was in the military sphere above all

others that Gustavus Adolphus left a lasting impression. In 1611 he was faced with a formidable task. The earlier Vasa kings, with the exception of John III, had endeavoured to improve the army, and Eric XIV had in fact initiated some original, though short-lived reforms. But Charles IX, no military leader, struggled against overwhelming difficulties and when he died the army lacked weapons, training, discipline, and above all, an effective organization. His son had been given a good theoretical instruction in the art of war, and he took advantage of the wars in Skåne, Ingria and Livonia to gain wide practical and technical experience which he later put to good use.

With regard to military organization, Gustavus Adolphus revised the system of conscription and in 1620 drew up new regulations for administration. He saw that as far as possible the army was paid regularly (which was very important for recruitment) by billeting soldiers and officers on farms, the rent of which, normally going to the Crown, they drew as their pay. By the time of the Prussian expedition, 1626, the main administrative and tactical unit of the infantry was the 'field-regiment' composed of two squadrons. The cavalry was by 1630 formed into squadrons and regiments, while in the previous year the first artillery regiment had been established. Moreover the King initiated great improvements in the equipment of his army. He rearmed the infantry with modern weapons, the pike and the musket, the design of both of which he had improved and, above all, he provided the artillery with new, lighter weapons, a reform which greatly influenced the rest of western Europe. Indeed the increased mobility and fire-power of Gustavus Adolphus's field-artillery gave him a tremendous advantage over his adversaries and transformed this aspect of warfare. Most important was the development of the famous 'regiment-piece', a new, light gun which could be drawn by one horse and thus moved about the field at will. Until this time the lightest guns had needed teams of up to nine horses and thus tended to remain ineffectively where they had been placed at the beginning of an engagement. In all his work of re-equipping his army, Gustavus Adolphus made full use of Sweden's capacity to support herself in munitions.

From the point of view of discipline, Protestant tradition has tended to exaggerate the 'godliness' of the Swedish soldier, and towards the end of the reign, despite the great efforts of the King to protect the civilian population, there was little to distinguish Swedish troops from the other nationalities fighting in Germany. None the less, training was kept at a high pitch: the troops were constantly exercised and engaged in manoeuvres, for effectiveness in battle depended on speed and precision.

Tactically Gustavus Adolphus revealed true genius. Not all his reforms were original or lasting, but he had the ability to select and amalgamate the best ideas from many contemporary experiments and in particular from those of Maurice of Orange. As a result he succeeded in endowing his army with remarkable mobility, a capacity for brilliant offensives, and the ability to remain strong in defence. At Breitenfeld in 1631, the enemy reeled under the new tactics employed by Gustavus Adolphus, who cleverly combined the different arms of his forces with truly dramatic effect. Instead of drawing up his infantry in an unwieldy mass in the centre of the field with the cavalry situated on the wings in contemporary fashion, Gustavus Adolphus interspersed blocks of infantry (pikemen and musketeers) with small squares of cavalry. Between these groups were detachments of musketeers ingeniously drawn up so that they could fire far more rapidly than their opponents. The rapidity of the volleys of the Swedish musketeers opened up gaps in the enemy ranks into which the cavalry or pikemen would charge, while the musketeers reloaded. When this was combined with the firing of the 'regiment-pieces', which could be sent into battle at the side of either the cavalry or the infantry and which were capable of being moved by only two men, the effect on the opposing masses, who were driven backwards in increasing disorder, was deadly. The King himself was notorious for disregarding his own safety and he took risks with his whole army which no contemporary commander would have contemplated. His judgment was not always sound, but the general brilliance of his manoeuvres far outweighed his occasional miscalculations. His tactical reforms made a lasting impression and his methods became models for subsequent European warfare. Napoleon selected only seven commanders in history whom he regarded as worthy of praise: Gustavus Adolphus's understanding of every aspect of warfare, from recruitment, drill, tactics and discipline, to his wide-ranging strategic plans, fully qualified him for his place in that list.

The navy

Military preoccupations did not result in a neglect of the navy, although Gustavus Adolphus's achievements in this sphere were far less dramatic. There were no naval battles of importance and tactically Sweden lagged behind the maritime nations of western Europe. But Gustavus Adolphus and Oxenstierna were well aware of Sweden's dependence on the fleet, a dependence which became more obvious as the years passed and Sweden's empire increased in size. In 1631 Oxenstierna wrote to Gustavus Adolphus:

It seems to me that it is essential that your Majesty should above all things labour to create a powerful fleet at sea; a fleet of good ships, and most especially a fleet very numerous, so that you may be master of every nook and cranny of the Baltic; and further that all sailors, and all that is used aboard ship, be before all else well maintained, and meetly and handsomely provided, so that the crews may be kept both in spirits and in health; even though this should mean leaving a regiment or two less on land.[4]

The recent war with Denmark, when Sweden's navy was powerless to prevent the Danes plundering trade and threatening invasion, when Älvsborg was captured and communications with the west threatened, brought home forcibly the need for the protection of a strong fleet. Sweden's developing export trade in minerals and timber had to be safeguarded, and the apparent danger from the Polish king, with his dynastic ambitions and growing fleet at Danzig, had to be countered. Later, Sweden's communications with the theatres of war, first in Livonia and Prussia, and then, above all, in Germany, had to be maintained;

4. *Rikslanseren Axel Oxenstiernas Skrifter och brelvaxling*, I, vi, 87. Quoted by Michael Roberts, op. cit.

troops, munitions and provisions had to be transported and tolls levied. The navy indeed played a most remarkable part in shipping Gustavus Adolphus's numerous forces abroad and in remaining at sea for long periods in all weathers to enforce the economic blockade along the southern and eastern coasts of the Baltic, a blockade so vital to Sweden. The empire which Sweden ultimately established in the Baltic was fundamentally maritime and it depended on the numerous naval stations placed along the coastlines of Swedish provinces and upon the warships patrolling the sea for its survival. The navy of Charles IX would have been totally inadequate to cope with such contingencies for, although he endeavoured to make some improvements after the appalling neglect of the previous reign, the fleet on his death in 1611 was small, ill-equipped and incompetent.

Fortunately Gustavus Adolphus understood most aspects of naval warfare, including the practical details of running a ship, and he made constant efforts to enlarge and re-equip the fleet and improve the efficiency of its administration. In Klas Fleming he found the greatest naval organizer Sweden had ever known. Advances were made in discipline and in the recruitment both of officers and ratings, and a central office of administration slowly took shape which in 1634 was finally established as one of the major organs of government. By 1632 the fleet was altogether larger, more modern and powerful than it had been twenty years earlier, and when Denmark and Sweden next met in combat upon the Baltic, the Swedes were more than a match for their old enemies.

The Church and education

But the achievements of Gustavus Adolphus were not all connected with such practical issues. In his dealings with the Church he showed a spirit of conciliation and encouragement very different from that of his father. In fact Charles IX had been suspected of Calvinism and there had been constant friction between the Crown and the leaders of the Church over ecclesiastical elections and administration. Gustavus Adolphus's aim of including

Church administration in the system of central government then being developed was defeated by determined opposition from the hierarchy, but in general a spirit of harmony and cooperation prevailed. Gustavus Adolphus gave his support to the printing of the Bible in 1618 and to the reformation of the Church in the Baltic provinces, while the Church loyally supported the Crown in carrying out its most important reforms. It was through the parish clergy that the Crown kept in touch with the people, and it was very much dependent on this support for obedience to its authority and for the enforcement of its measures. Moreover, fundamentally the Crown and the Church were dependent on each other's support for their security. Any political threat to Gustavus Adolphus from Sigismund III of Poland represented also the danger of Roman Catholicism to the Lutheran Church. Thus the ferocious Statute of Örebro against Roman Catholics in 1617 was really a measure against Polish political activity. Roman Catholicism was never a serious danger to the Swedish Church unless imposed by force, and from 1617 onward (the year also of Gustavus Adolphus's coronation) the threat from Poland and the Swedish exiles both to Church and State declined as the years passed.

The King also devoted much time and thought to Sweden's educational system. By his establishment of *gymnasia*, or high-schools to provide a secondary education in preparation for the university, in his attempts to combat illiteracy and raise the educational standards of the clergy, encouraging them in their duty to teach in the parishes, and by his efforts to liberalize and widen the curriculum, Gustavus Adolphus did much for the educational welfare of his country. Above all towers his work for the University of Uppsala. This ancient seat of learning had disintegrated at the time of Sweden's independence and Swedish scholars became dependent on German Protestant universities for their higher education. The University of Uppsala was re-founded in 1593 but throughout Charles IX's reign it suffered from incompetent organization, was torn by internal feuds, and was hampered by lack of finance. Gustavus Adolphus did much to solve the problem of internal strife and he gave the university

generous grants of property. A constitution with regular officers
under a chancellor was drawn up and the subject-matter to be
pursued in the newly established faculties was defined. Gustavus
Adolphus met with determined opposition in many of his educational schemes and when he died in 1632 a great deal remained
to be done. But, as his biographer, Professor Roberts, comments:

It is not easy to think of a seventeenth-century monarch whose
services to education are fit to be drawn into comparison with his.[5]

[15] SWEDEN IN 1620

By 1620 Gustavus Adolphus was in a much more secure position
both at home and abroad. The danger of invasion from Poland
had receded and neither side was able to make progress in the
brief war which broke out in 1617. In that year also the peace of
Stolbovo, between Sweden and Russia, brought for Sweden a
very satisfactory end to a long and exhausting struggle. Ingria
and Estonia were secured; Russia was cut off from the Baltic; the
Gulf of Finland was now a 'Swedish stream', and any attack
contemplated by Poland by way of Finland was far less feasible.
In 1620 Gustavus Adolphus married Maria Eleonora, daughter
of the Elector John Sigismund of Brandenburg and, although it
was not followed by the hoped-for alliance, it registered a diplomatic triumph over Sigismund III. In the west, the peace of
Knäred in 1613 had ended the war with Denmark and, on the
face of it, was a serious reverse for Sweden. But Christian IV had
been forced to relinquish his hopes of conquering Sweden and
recreating the union of the Scandinavian states, and Sweden had
at least maintained her exemption from the Sound dues. Sweden,
indeed, had survived, and the next years saw a strengthening of
her diplomatic position. The Dutch had been antagonized by the
apparent strength of Denmark in the Sound and in the Baltic in
general, and in 1614 they made an alliance with Sweden. Lübeck

5. Michael Roberts, op. cit.

was already allied to the Netherlands and soon other important Hanse towns in north Germany joined them; the latter also felt themselves to be menaced by Denmark whose king was clearly aiming at establishing his sons in the secularized bishoprics and at controlling the Weser and the Elbe, important commercial highways. Sweden, therefore, after a decade of Gustavus Adolphus's rule, was no longer at the mercy of her neighbours. But it soon became increasingly evident that her search for security in the north had in fact only just begun; a search which was to become entangled with the great religious and political struggle at this very time gathering momentum in Germany and known henceforth as the Thirty Years' War; a search moreover, which was to lead Sweden into paths of unforeseen greatness.

[16] THE THIRTY YEARS' WAR

Confusion and crisis in Germany

That the situation in Germany was becoming critical had been evident for many years before the famous 'defenestration of Prague' signalled the outbreak of war in 1618. The Holy Roman Empire presented a welter of confused ambitions both religious and political: Catholics were arrayed against Protestants, Lutherans against Calvinists, princes against the Emperor, and prince against prince. Foreign powers, enlisted as allies, found in Germany the means of satisfying their own ambitions: the Austrian Habsburgs relied on their Spanish kinsmen to help them enforce their absolutist schemes and to spread the Catholic faith, while the princes turned this way and that, to Protestant Denmark and Sweden, or to Catholic France, in their endeavours to preserve their religion and their 'liberties'. The Catholic Maximilian of Bavaria found himself torn between furthering the religious policy of the Emperor and, in alliance with France, opposing the political aims of the Habsburg dynasty. The Lutheran John

George of Saxony, loyal to the traditions of the Empire, supported
the Habsburgs against what he considered to be the illegal actions
of Frederick, the Calvinist Elector of the Palatinate, in accepting
the Bohemian crown. Furthermore, resenting foreign influence in
Germany, he refused for a long while to support the 'Protestant
Hero', in the person of Gustavus Adolphus, despite the increasing
success of the Catholic armies in central and northern Germany.
The leading princes, Maximilian, John George, and George
William of Brandenburg (a Calvinist), were thus prevented by
their several religions from working together, either to oppose
the absolutism of the Habsburgs, a policy pursued with vigour by
the Emperor Ferdinand II, or to prevent foreign interference
within the Empire. On the other hand, Ferdinand, in his efforts
to restore the power of the Catholic Church, could not rely on the
Catholic princes to support him, and the Protestants, divided
among themselves, were unable effectively to defend their faith,
whether Lutheran or Calvinist. In short everyone was at cross
purposes, with the possible exception of the Emperor, and events
in Germany moved rapidly from one complicated crisis to another.

By the beginning of the seventeenth century, the Counter-
Reformation had made great gains in Germany and in 1607 the
Catholic princes demanded that all land secularized since 1552
should be restored to the Church. This date, laid down by the
religious peace of Augsburg in 1555, allowed the Lutherans (the
Calvinists were not included) those lands which had been secularized up to that year but permitted no more to be taken from the
Church. The peace had not been adhered to and by 1600 much
more land had been secularized both by Lutheran and Calvinist
princes. In fact the demand of 1607 would have resulted in little
short of a revolution. In face of this danger, certain Protestant
princes joined together in 1608 in an Evangelical Union under the
leadership of Frederick, the Elector of the Palatinate. The following year a Catholic League was formed with Maximilian of
Bavaria at its head, and a general war seemed imminent over the
disputed ownership of the duchies of Cleves and Jülich. For the
time however it was averted.

The outbreak of war and the entry of Sweden into the struggle

The spark which set Europe alight was to come from Bohemia, a Habsburg territory outside the Empire with a strong Protestant tradition. When the Bohemians saw their religious liberty threatened first by the Emperor Matthias, and then, even more dangerously by Ferdinand II, they took matters into their own hands, rebelled against the Habsburg dynasty, and in 1619 offered the crown to the Elector of the Palatinate. The latter's acceptance horrified many princes in Germany, in particular John George, and it soon became clear that there was no hope of a united Protestant front. John George, indeed, sent troops to help the Emperor, who also gained Maximilian's support in return for the promise of Frederick's Electorate. The Protestant Union was weak and no help was to be expected from France, beset with internal difficulties, or, it soon became apparent, from James I of England (Frederick's father-in-law) who pursued the most unrealistic policies. The Dutch, on the point of renewed war with Spain, felt themselves able to send financial aid only. Thus in 1620 Frederick was driven out of Bohemia where Protestantism was harshly stamped out, and his electorate overrun by Spanish and Bavarian troops. The next year the Protestant Union dissolved in confusion and the cause of the Counter-Reformation appeared triumphant. Gustavus Adolphus, watching from the side-lines, foresaw the growing danger to Protestantism from the Catholic armies, and in 1621 he wrote to Adolf Frederick of Mecklenburg: 'Hodie illi, cras tibi'.

But the Protestant princes seemed unwilling to make any efforts to protect themselves and, as neither Sweden in particular nor the Baltic in general was at this time threatened by the Habsburgs or their allies, the time was not yet ripe for intervention from Scandinavia. Gustavus Adolphus concentrated on domestic and military reform and on his long-standing war with Poland. In 1621 he reopened that struggle by capturing Riga, which had the reputation of being one of the strongest fortresses in the north and which was well known to the maritime powers.

Europe was thus forced to recognize the emergence of Sweden as a power to be reckoned with in the Baltic. At this point it seems that Gustavus Adolphus was willing to abandon his gains in Livonia in return for a guarantee by Sigismund that he would cease his propaganda and relinquish his claim to the Swedish throne. But it was a vain hope, and in 1622 another truce was made. The following year saw a plan put forward by Gustavus Adolphus for a Protestant League in Germany, supported if necessary by Swedish arms, but he proposed that Sweden should make her chief contribution by attacking Poland and then threatening the Habsburg dominions in the south. This proposal came to nothing but it showed that Gustavus Adolphus was by no means unmindful of events in Germany.

Relations with Denmark were again extremely bad, irritation caused in particular by Danish ambitions in north Germany, and war seemed imminent. But in 1624, after negotiations, Christian IV gave way on all important points, a fact which bore witness to the changing balance of power in the Baltic. Sweden was no longer militarily inferior to her rival; Gustavus Adolphus's reforms were producing their effects. However it was Denmark and not Sweden who now seized the leadership of the Protestants in Europe and Christian IV put himself at the head of an army against the triumphant imperialist forces in Germany. On the other hand Gustavus Adolphus had refused to agree to any plan of intervention which did not fully guarantee Sweden's safety in the Baltic, and his stringent demands were regarded as too high. Thus he turned again to Livonia which by 1626 was finally secured.

But it was in Prussia that Gustavus Adolphus now hoped to defeat Sigismund's pretensions once and for all. The capture of Poland's only outlet to the Baltic and the disruption of her valuable trade through Danzig and other ports would be a most devastating blow. Furthermore, from Prussia, Gustavus Adolphus could keep a closer eye on the progress of the Thirty Years' War. The situation for the Protestants was becoming increasingly serious. Denmark was making no headway against the Imperialists, who were moving steadily northwards. At the same time rumours of

Spanish plans for control of the Baltic and for establishing naval contact with Sigismund were alarming. Thus in the summer of 1626 Gustavus Adolphus captured the important port of Pillau in East Prussia; his brother-in-law, George William, described by Sir Thomas Roe as 'a grayne of corne betweene two millstones, brused to make bread for others', was unable to resist. Polish opposition in Prussia proved unexpectedly determined but the improvements in Swedish arms and tactics were really apparent for the first time. Meanwhile in August Denmark was decisively defeated at Lutter and the imperialist armies, under their un- scrupulous but skilful commander Wallenstein, moved into Mecklenburg and Pomerania on the Baltic coast and ravaged Jutland. An invasion of Denmark seemed at hand, and with Wallenstein's capture of Wismar, an imperial naval base on the Baltic became only a matter of time. Moreover 1627 saw the first of Wallenstein's regiments dispatched to help Sigismund. In November Gustavus Adolphus wrote to Oxenstierna that Sweden's participation in the war in Germany could not be delayed much longer and he received emphatic backing in his views from the Riksdag.

Under these circumstances it was understandable that the Scandinavian struggle for *dominium* in the Baltic should be temporarily in abeyance and that Denmark and Sweden should unite against the common enemy. In 1628 a treaty was made and a joint expedition saved Stralsund from capture by Wallenstein (now named 'Generalissimo of the Oceanic and Baltic Seas' by the Emperor), who had found Wismar unsuitable as a naval base. In fact, however, Denmark was anxious for peace, Christian IV's Council having washed their hands of their king's actions, and as a result of the treaty of Lübeck in May 1629 between Denmark and the Emperor, Sweden was left to act alone. With the media- tion of France the Swedo-Polish war came to an end in the Truce of Altmark in 1629, which guaranteed to Sweden the valuable tolls she had been levying along the Prussian coast. In Germany Gustavus Adolphus was already looked upon as the saviour of Protestantism, although no prince had as yet come out firmly in his favour, nor had negotiations with France resulted in a satis-

factory agreement. But in March 1630, fears that Denmark was
intriguing with Wallenstein over the possession of the important
island of Rügen, led Gustavus Adolphus to intervene there and
expel the Imperialists. In June 1630 his army landed at Peene-
münde in Pomerania and the invasion of Germany had begun.

The motives of Gustavus Adolphus

Gustavus Adolphus's motives for entering the Thirty Years' War
have been the subject of controversy ever since. Was he impelled
by religious idealism or by the requirements of nationalistic
politics; was he the Protestant hero or the Swedish aggressor?
Our great difficulty is to appreciate the way in which seventeenth-
century thought equated politics and religion. Thus a threat to
Swedish Lutheranism was also a threat to national independence.
Politics and religion were not kept in watertight compartments,
and Gustavus Adolphus was undoubtedly strongly influenced by
both considerations. He saw himself as the Protestant hero;
he believed in his mission and was sincerely anxious to help the
oppressed Protestants in Germany. His later schemes, intended to
safeguard the faith on the continent, set him apart from the
majority of the protagonists in that struggle, protagonists openly
pursuing their own selfish ends. Certainly the cause of Protestantism had a lot to thank him for. But when this is said, there is
ample justification for Miss C. V. Wedgwood's[6] comment that
Gustavus Adolphus had a great capacity for self-deception. Consequently it was not until he began to feel seriously threatened
by the growing prospect of Habsburg control over the Baltic
that he actually intervened, although Protestantism in Germany
had been at low ebb for the past decade, and throughout the
ensuing struggle he never for one moment lost sight of his country's interests. In short he was not a fanatic; he was not a crusader.
He was a far-sighted practical statesman, and, in the long run,
he saw everything through Swedish eyes. Since 1611 he had
devoted himself to building up Sweden's position in the north,
to strengthening his country internally and economically, to

6. C. V. Wedgwood, *The Thirty Years' War*, Penguin (Harmondsworth, 1957).

removing the threat from Russia, defeating the ambitions of Denmark, resolving the dynastic conflict with Poland, and to making Sweden a maritime and naval power to be reckoned with. By 1630 these aims were in many ways achieved, but now on the southern Baltic coast a new factor had arisen which could no longer be ignored. The Habsburgs were making a bid for power in the north: the Baltic coastlands had been overrun, Jutland invaded, and a navy, which could threaten the trade and security of Scandinavia, was being constructed. In addition the Emperor was acting as the instrument of the Counter-Reformation and had made great gains at the expense of German Protestantism. He was allied to Spain and was intriguing with Sigismund of Poland. What could be more logical than that Sweden, led by a king in temperament well-suited to a dynamic policy, should counter this threat by pushing the Imperialists back from the Baltic coast and presenting henceforth a barrier to their religious and political ambitions? In 1630 Gustavus Adolphus had no great schemes of Swedish domination or of remodelling the Empire. He progressed from expedient to expedient, his moves dictated by the turn of events and by military necessity. The needs of German Protestantism and Sweden's national security and pro- gress in the north had coincided. Gustavus Adolphus saw himself, as did the average German Protestant, as the champion of the faith; in fact, without denying his genuine concern for Protes- tantism, his duty to Sweden always came first.

Gustavus Adolphus in Germany, 1630–2

The situation in Germany in 1630 had recently become more favourable to foreign intervention. The Emperor Ferdinand in 1629 had at last published the Edict of Restitution reinstating the Catholics in the secularized lands and thus alienating the Protestant princes, above all Saxony and Brandenburg. More- over the dismissal of Wallenstein by the Emperor removed by far the most able commander that Gustavus Adolphus would have to meet, and a secret agreement between France and Bavaria represented the virtual desertion of Ferdinand by the Catholic

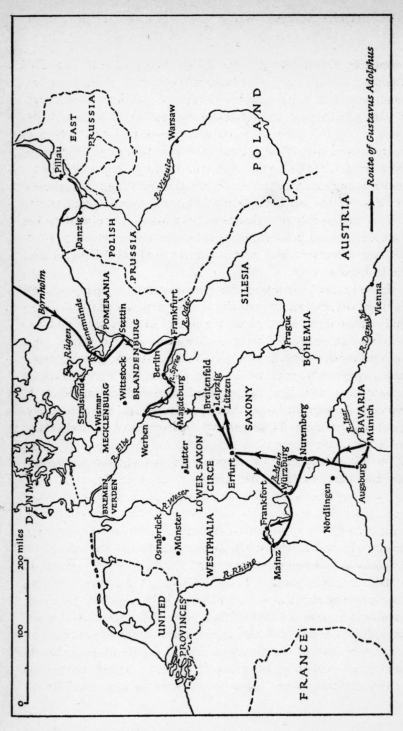

GUSTAVUS ADOLPHUS IN GERMANY, 1630–2

League. In July 1630 Gustavus Adolphus captured Stettin and
advanced steadily along the Oder without meeting very serious
resistance. But neither John George of Saxony nor George
William of Brandenburg would abandon their middle course and
make a firm alliance with Sweden, although in January 1631 a
treaty was at last signed between Sweden and France. Richelieu
had hoped to make Gustavus Adolphus his willing tool and to
force him to guarantee the neutrality of Bavaria and the League,
who figured strongly in Richelieu's plans for establishing a party
against the Habsburgs. But Gustavus Adolphus refused to be
manipulated and in fact the Treaty of Bärwalde, which granted
large subsidies to Sweden, went a long way to forcing Bavaria into
the Habsburg camp.

Early in 1631 Gustavus Adolphus overran a large area of
Mecklenburg, but the capture by the Imperialists of the strategically situated city of Magdeburg, where the Protestants had been
encouraged to rebel with promises of immediate Swedish aid, was
a severe blow. Gustavus Adolphus had wasted valuable time endeavouring to persuade the Electors of Saxony and Brandenburg
to cooperate with him, and in May the city was sacked with
appalling ferocity. Although the responsibility for this catastrophe
is not wholly Gustavus Adolphus's, he does not emerge from this
sad affair with much credit.

The fall of Magdeburg profoundly affected the rest of Protestant Germany. In June 1631 George William was forced to sign
an agreement with Sweden, and the other leading Protestant
princes, notably those of Hesse-Cassel and Saxe-Weimar, found
themselves driven to rely on Gustavus Adolphus. But it was John
George who was needed most. His electorate was well-placed in
Germany and he had comparatively large forces at his command.
At last, in September 1631, John George, threatened with invasion by the imperialist forces under Tilly, another able commander, and with the loss of his secularized lands, threw in his
lot with Gustavus Adolphus. In the same month the imperialist
forces were overwhelmed in the famous battle of Breitenfeld,
fought on 7 September near Leipzig. It was a victory won by the
Swedes fighting under Gustavus Adolphus's new methods of

tactics and discipline, and a really resounding defeat for their opponents whose losses may have been as many as 20,000 men, while the Swedish dead and captured were estimated as only 2,100.

Germany was now open to Gustavus Adolphus and much controversy surrounds his decision to march to the Rhineland rather than Vienna. From this time onwards his strategy is not as carefully thought-out and executed: he began to take considerable risks and a certain pride and arrogance crept into his behaviour. In fact his best plan after Breitenfeld would have been to pursue Tilly's army into the region of the Lower Saxon Circle and destroy it completely: he was to live to regret this omission. But for the time he made triumphant progress towards Mainz where he spent the winter of 1631–2. Communications with Sweden were thus stretched to the utmost, and the supply of finance, provisions and recruits, both from home and in Germany, constituted an enormous administrative problem. Furthermore the danger from Spain could not be ignored; Tilly's forces were making a remarkable recovery, while Richelieu was watching the progress of his ally with some alarm.

Already, in a document drawn up in April 1631, *Norma Futurarum Actionum*, Gustavus Adolphus had visualized a league of German princes, with himself at the head, to safeguard Protestantism. He had also concluded that Pomerania would have to remain Swedish at the end of the war as security and compensation for Sweden. Early in 1632 the scheme for a permanent Protestant League, with an effective leader and military strength, was given more definite shape, and by this time Gustavus Adolphus clearly believed that a really enduring settlement needed the guarantee of Swedish leadership. It was certainly true that the German princes seemed incapable of working together for the good of their faith, but Gustavus Adolphus took little account of the fact that they might object to being saved in spite of themselves. In June 1632 at Nuremberg he argued that there must be in Germany a *corpus bellicum* to conduct the war and a *corpus politicum* or *evangelicum* to preserve the peace, and it is evident that Sweden was to command both. These schemes were in the long run quite impractical, for the German princes would never have agreed to foreign interference on such a scale. In fact Gustavus Adolphus had already resorted to violence in order to force them into line and only his premature death saved him from ultimate disillusionment. But in all these plans and endeavours there is little evidence that Gustavus Adolphus ever aspired to a radical reorganization of the constitution of the Empire, or that he ever dreamed of ascending the imperial throne despite the fact that the latter possibility was canvassed throughout contemporary Europe.

From his position on the Rhine, Gustavus Adolphus recruited and planned his enormous armies for the campaign of 1632. An attack on Vienna was to be made by way of the Danube, Bavaria having been defeated first. In order to accomplish this, John George must hold his position in Saxony and Silesia; the Imperialists in the Lower Saxon Circle must be wiped out, and at the same time the Rhine must be securely held. But Gustavus Adolphus soon met serious opposition. In December 1631 Wallenstein was once again appointed to lead the forces of the Emperor and he set about raising large forces in Bohemia and, much to Gustavus's anxiety, intriguing with Saxony. Another superior commander, Pappenheim, defeated all attempts to crush imperial resistance in the Lower Saxon Circle and constantly menaced the Swedish rear and the communications from central Germany to the Baltic. Meanwhile the conquest of Bavaria proceeded successfully, although Gustavus Adolphus failed in his aim of drawing Wallenstein's army away from Bohemia and Saxony. In fact it was Wallenstein's successes in Bohemia which drew Gustavus Adolphus away from Bavaria. The two armies met in July at Nuremberg and remained facing each other for nearly two months, Gustavus Adolphus on the defensive and Wallenstein in a remarkably strong position. Gustavus Adolphus's eventual attack was repulsed and he marched once more to the Danube. He was soon forced to return, for Wallenstein had invaded Saxony and was inflicting great damage. Leipzig was captured at the end of October but Wallenstein delivered himself to the enemy when, mistakenly imagining that Gustavus Adolphus had gone into winter quarters, he began to disperse his forces. On 6 November 1632, at Lützen (again near Leipzig), Gustavus Adolphus fell upon the unprepared imperial troops and, after a bloody battle in which Gustavus Adolphus met his death, the Swedes won the day. The loss of their king spurred them to great efforts under the skilful leadership of Bernard of Saxe-Weimar, but it was a hollow victory. They had lost their great inspiration, and once the personal magnetism exercised by Gustavus Adolphus was gone there was little left to hold together the heterogeneous mass of soldiers fighting under the Swedish flag. Indeed there was little left either of the Protestant cause.

The war continues: Sweden defeats Denmark, 1645

Oxenstierna, who had worked with the king through all his difficulties and who had such an intimate knowledge of German affairs, was obviously the only person fit to carry on the government of Sweden on the death of Gustavus Adolphus. The new Queen was only six, and the Queen Mother was most unstable. Thus the Council of Regency, consisting of the five most important state officials, was dominated by Oxenstierna and his family. For the next decade he ruled the country with a firm hand and every branch of the administration felt his watchful eye. Trade and industry were promoted, and Sweden's military and naval strength maintained. It was not until Queen Christina came of age in 1644 that his authority was gradually undermined. It was the Queen's determination for an early peace, and her interference in the negotiations, which probably reduced Sweden's ultimate gains. But while the war continued, Christina knew that she could not dispense with the able Chancellor.

During the four years immediately following Gustavus Adolphus's death, Oxenstierna remained in Germany where he was faced with almost superhuman tasks. Besides the pressing problems of war administration, he had to conduct intricate negotiations with cunning or feckless allies, to compose the differences between his ambitious generals, and above all he had to maintain some control and discipline in an army consisting of native Swedes and

mutinous mercenaries of many nationalities. Moreover Oxenstierna was constantly working against the growing influence of
France in German affairs, and he needed all his diplomatic skill
to prevent Sweden's position from being undermined altogether.
In short the situation in Germany needed a man of great and
various ability, a man of patience, tenacity and courage; it was
providential for Sweden that Oxenstierna was such a man.

In 1633 he presided over a meeting of some of the German
Protestant princes at Heilbronn. This was the first real attempt
to carry out Gustavus Adolphus's principle of establishing a
corpus to defend the Protestant cause, and it was hoped that
similar leagues would be set up elsewhere in Germany. But
France, fearing that Sweden would thus become too influential,
set herself to detach the Protestant princes one by one. Disaster
ultimately overwhelmed the Heilbronn League after the decisive
defeat of Swedish forces at Nördlingen in 1634. With the definitive entry of France into the war in 1635 as the avowed enemy
of the Habsburgs, the cause of religion, whether Catholic or
Protestant, began to fade. Its place was filled more and more by
militant nationalism. For his part, Oxenstierna was determined
that Sweden should obtain considerable territorial compensation
in Germany for her sacrifices during the war and, until a peace
could be made which guaranteed such satisfaction, there was
little hope that Sweden would evacuate German territory.

Despite many difficulties, Swedish troops under a series of
able commanders, Saxe-Weimar, Horn, Baner, Torstensson and
Wrangel, more than held their own during the remaining years
of the war. 1635 saw the final loss of Saxony who, followed by
many other leading princes, made the Treaty of Prague with the
Emperor, by which the latter abandoned the Edict of Restitution.
In the same year the renewal of the Truce of Altmark for twenty-
six years with Poland resulted in Sweden relinquishing the valuable Prussian tolls. In 1636 Oxenstierna returned to Sweden
where he directed the dispatch of supplies with a firm hand. A
conspicuous success for Swedish arms was won at Wittstock in
Brandenburg and the war was swiftly carried into the heart of
Habsburg territory. In 1642 Swedish troops under Torstensson

inflicted a second heavy defeat on imperialist troops at Breitenfeld, and in the following year Sweden even found the strength
to prosecute a successful war against Denmark.

Thus Torstensson was ordered to evacuate Habsburg territory
and to move north into Schleswig-Holstein. At the same time
another Swedish army invaded Skåne. Christian IV, jealous of
Sweden's position in Europe, had made every effort to thwart his
neighbour. He offered to mediate in the peace negotiations between Sweden and the Emperor, a mediator in whom Sweden
could hardly place much confidence; he assisted the Swedish
Queen Mother to fly her country; his son had married the daughter of the Elector of Saxony, now firmly attached to the Emperor,
and he was still scheming for the north German bishoprics. The
immediate cause for war was his attempt to limit Sweden's
exemption from the Sound dues by refusing to include in that
exemption any territory which Sweden had acquired since the
peace of Knäred of 1613. Thus Christian found himself engaged
in a disastrous war for which he was totally unprepared. Swedish
troops swiftly overran Skåne and Jutland and were only prevented by the Danish navy from invading the islands. By 1644
Denmark was completely defeated. At the peace of Brömsebro
1645, Sweden was guaranteed unrestricted exemption from the
Sound dues, and Denmark surrendered the strategic islands of
Ösel and Gotland as well as the Norwegian provinces of Jämtland
and Härjedalen. Furthermore Sweden was to occupy Halland
for thirty years as a guarantee that these provisions would be
faithfully adhered to. This was for Denmark a most humiliating
peace and registered a complete reversal of the balance of power
in the Baltic. Denmark could no longer claim to be the master of
that sea, while Sweden had not only broken out of her former
encirclement by Denmark, but had begun herself to encroach
on Danish territory. Indeed the time was not far distant when
Denmark would, in her turn, feel the threat of encirclement. As
early as June 1632 the King of Sweden had made overtures to the
Duke of Holstein-Gottorp, and this connexion was later to be a
constant source of friction between the two Scandinavian powers.

Meanwhile in Germany Torstensson again turned southwards

and invaded Bohemia, and during the last years of the war his successor, Wrangel, in cooperation with France, invaded Bavaria, and inflicted serious defeats on the forces of the Emperor. When peace was signed in 1648, after years of negotiation, the Swedes were storming Prague, the city which had seen the beginning of the war thirty years earlier.

The Peace of Westphalia, 1648

The terms of the Peace of Westphalia were finally agreed at Osnabrück, between Sweden and the Emperor, and at Münster, between France and the Emperor, thus avoiding difficulties of diplomatic precedence. Sweden had to abandon her hopes of Silesia, but she acquired, as imperial fiefs, Western Pomerania including the important port of Stettin on the river Oder, the port of Wismar in Mecklenburg, and the bishoprics of Bremen and Verden, so dear to the heart of Christian IV. After so many years and such great exertions these gains appear somewhat meagre, but Sweden in fact occupied an influential position in the Empire as well as controlling the three most important rivers in north Germany. Among other provisions made in the peace, the Calvinists were included in the general religious settlement and 1 January 1624 was taken as the day of restitution for secularized lands. The peace registered the fact that the Habsburgs had failed either to make the Empire a powerful force, or to extend the influence of the Counter-Reformation throughout Germany.

[17] SWEDEN'S DOMINANCE IN 1648

By 1648 Sweden's position among the powers had thus been revolutionized. She was recognized as the foremost Protestant power and the leading military power in Europe. Denmark's domination in the Baltic had been broken, and in the bishoprics of Bremen and Verden Sweden had acquired territories strategically placed to the south of her old rival. The dynastic quarrel with Poland

SWEDISH TERRITORIAL GAINS BY **1648**

had not yet been finally resolved, but that declining power no
longer presented any danger. The Gulf of Finland was Swedish
from shore to shore, Denmark had been divested of Gotland and
Ösel, and long stretches of valuable Baltic coastline, Livonia and
Western Pomerania, were in Swedish hands. In fact Sweden was
probably the power most feared in Europe in the years immediately following the Thirty Years' War. But this fear was not
really justified and a closer look at Sweden's position in 1648 will
reveal serious weaknesses, weaknesses which were to present the
successors of Gustavus Adolphus and Oxenstierna with ever-
increasing problems both in domestic and foreign affairs, and
which go a long way to explain the course of Swedish history
during the rest of the century.

The architects of Sweden's greatness were undeniably Gustavus
Adolphus and his Chancellor Oxenstierna, but it must not be
overlooked that the international situation during these years
was not unfavourable. Not only were France and England pre-
occupied with internal difficulties and Spain and the Dutch at
war, but Sweden's immediate neighbours showed signs of temporary or permanent decline. Thus Denmark, Sweden's most
serious rival both for power in the Baltic and for the leadership
of the Protestant world, was in fact in no position to challenge,
and steadily grew weaker. Under Christian IV, whose majestic
appearance and kingly pursuits were hailed with delight by his
subjects, Denmark indeed was not neglected. The King showed
great energy, intelligence and courage in improving his country's
defences, stimulating trade and industry, founding new towns
and enlarging old ones, rebuilding the navy, and transforming
Copenhagen into a thriving capital city filled with noble buildings.
But Christian tended to pursue several contradictory policies at
once, often exhibiting short-sightedness, a lack of caution and
self-control. He alienated the maritime powers, his potential
allies, by raising the Sound dues, while plunging ill-prepared into
a war with Sweden. Again, he attempted to pursue an aggressive
policy in north Germany but failed to create an army which
would have given the necessary weight to his demands. Indeed
Christian would have engaged in frequent military enterprises

had not the Council refused to support him, thereby, no doubt, saving Denmark from even greater humiliations. He was thus no match for Gustavus Adolphus.

But the fundamental weakness of Denmark was social. For many years the nobility had been crystallizing into an irresponsible, self-seeking, exclusive caste, with ever widening social and economic privileges. Simultaneously the middle classes and the peasants were trodden underfoot. The contrast with the position in Sweden, where the independent peasantry and the thriving business and mercantile community were a great source of strength, needs no pointing. Moreover the Danish monarchy was elective and its power was strictly limited by the Council composed of the great nobles. The relationship between Christian IV and his Council deteriorated seriously throughout the reign and the latter refused to carry out its financial and military responsibilities. The Danish king, unlike Gustavus Adolphus, failed to come to terms with the problem of the nobles and even increased their power by marrying his daughters to the leaders of that class. Under these circumstances Christian found it impossible to construct an efficient, well-equipped army, and the situation was made worse by the ravages of invading troops, first Imperialists and then Swedes. In 1648, after five of the most disastrous years in Danish history, Christian IV died, a broken man.

In Poland the reigns of Sigismund III and his elder son Ladislas (1632–48) form a prelude to the subsequent complete dislocation of the state. Until 1648 Poland was still accorded the rank of a great power and had come to be regarded as the barricade of Christendom against the Turks. During the 'Time of Troubles' in Russia, Poland had made great gains and between 1632 and 1634 she succeeded in repulsing Russia's endeavours to recover her lost territory. But serious internal weaknesses were becoming more and more pronounced. The ancient commercial prosperity of Polish cities was decaying rapidly in the face of legislation which was purely to the advantage of the landed class: the peasants were reduced to serfdom and the nobles increased in privilege and lawlessness. It has been estimated that one in ten of the population were nobles, and this class monopolized all

property and power in the state. The Diet was composed not of
the different estates but solely of the nobles (admittedly often
poor, with little land), while the great magnates controlled all the
important offices. They limited the power of the King, and the
elective nature of the monarchy (which had been finally established in 1573) was soon to be an excuse for factious rivalry and
foreign intervention. Gradually, also, the legislative authority
in the state was declining; the increasing insistence on unanimity
in the Diet stultified government and restricted reform. The
Jesuits controlled the Church and the presence of other religions
and nationalities made for internal dissension. Military weakness
was more and more evident as the nobles in their efforts to curb
monarchical power kept the King short of money and made the
financing of an efficient army impossible. Externally the threat
from Russia was growing and in the background there was always
the menace of Turkey. Moreover, although for the time the Poles
were able to suppress the efforts of the Cossacks on the river
Dnieper to set up an independent state, their ultimate failure to
cope with this problem brought disaster to the last Vasa King of
Poland, John Casimir, who succeeded his brother in 1648.

Russia in 1613 also presented a picture of disintegration.
Economically and financially she was impoverished; much of the
land had been ravaged during the 'Time of Troubles', and the
old Muscovite militia was shown to be quite inadequate in the
face of western armies. A policy of defence and reconstruction
was necessary, and the first Romanov czars, Michael (1613–45)
and Alexis (1645–76), concentrated on internal consolidation and,
in particular, on military reform. The government engaged
western experts and instructors to remodel the army, and western capital was also attracted to Russia; when rich iron ore de-
posits were discovered their exploitation was undertaken by a
Dutch merchant, Andrei Vinius. The years 1632–4 saw humiliating defeats by Poland, although the latter was finally forced to
renounce all pretension to the Russian throne, but this was destined to be the last time Russia would submit to her neighbour.
The Cossack rebels, seeking Muscovite help against the Poles,
initiated the expansion of Russia at Poland's expense. Ultimately

Sweden would also fall a victim, but such a possibility must have been far from the minds of men who had just witnessed Sweden's glories.

During the first half of the seventeenth century, therefore, Sweden had little to fear from her immediate neighbours in the north. She had even less need, it seemed, to take into account the weak and scattered electorate of Brandenburg-Prussia. The Elector George William (1619–40) had followed a vacillating policy throughout the Thirty Years' War, fearing the ambitions of Sweden, Poland and the Habsburgs, and wishing to remain neutral but not strong enough to enforce that neutrality. His various territories were consequently devastated and the fortunes of Brandenburg-Prussia reached a low ebb. Internally the power of the Elector continued to decline in favour of the local Estates, and thus, with no effective military force, George William was unable to prevent either invasion by the foreigner or domination by the nobles. But the accession in 1640 of the Elector Frederick William, who was determined not to play a similarly helpless role, heralded a new era in the history of the electorate. The acquisition at the Peace of Westphalia of Eastern Pomerania, Magdeburg, Halberstadt, Kammin and Minden, emphasized the fact that, with the earlier additions in 1618 of East Prussia and the Rhine duchies of Cleves, Mark and Ravensberg, the first half of the seventeenth century had actually been a period of considerable territorial expansion for Brandenberg. Moreover, the loss to Sweden at the same peace of a valuable part of Pomerania, and the fear of that power's ambitions in Polish Prussia, meant that henceforth the Great Elector could be numbered among Sweden's enemies. Underestimation of the capabilities of Frederick William and the potentialities of Brandenburg-Prussia was a constant though understandable flaw in subsequent Swedish policy.

Principal Events, 1611 – 48

SWEDEN AND THE BALTIC POWERS

1611
Accession of Gustavus Adolphus

1612
Charter presented to Gustavus Adolphus by nobles

1613
Peace of Knäred between Sweden and Denmark

1617
Riksdag Ordinance. Statute of Örebro. Peace of Stolbovo between Sweden and Russia

1626
Livonia secured by Sweden. Prussian expedition

1629
Truce of Altmark between Sweden and Poland

THE THIRTY YEARS' WAR

1618
Outbreak of Thirty Years' War

1625
Denmark enters war

1626
Defeat of Denmark at battle of Lutter. Imperialists under Wallenstein overrun the Baltic coastlands

1628
Joint Dano-Swedish expedition to save Stralsund

1629
Denmark retires from war

1630
Gustavus Adolphus lands
in Germany

1631
Treaty of Bärwalde between
France and Sweden. Fall
of Magdeburg
7 September. Battle of
Breitenfeld

1632
Regency government in
Sweden

1632
6 November. Battle of
Lützen
Death of Gustavus
Adolphus

1633
Heilbronn League

1634
Form of Government

1634
Battle of Nördlingen

1635
Twenty-six years' truce
between Sweden and
Poland

1635
France enters Thirty Years'
War

1643
Outbreak of war between
Sweden and Denmark

1644
Queen Christina comes of age

1645
Peace of Brömsebro between
Sweden and Denmark

1648
Peace of Westphalia: the end
of the Thirty Years' War

Further Reading

MICHAEL ROBERTS, *Gustavus Adolphus: History of Sweden, 1611–1632,* 2 vols. Longmans (London, 1953).

C. V. WEDGWOOD, *The Thirty Years' War.* Penguin (Harmondsworth, 1957).

S. H. STEINBERG, *The Thirty Years' War and the Conflict for European Hegemony* 1600–1660. Edward Arnold (London, 1966).

MICHAEL ROBERTS, *Gustavas Adolphus and the Rise of Sweden.* English Universities Press (London, 1973).

See also pages 44-5.

PART IV
The Northern Wars—Sweden's Baltic Empire at its Height

The years from the Peace of Westphalia, 1648, to the northern wars, 1655–60, form a significant period in the history of the struggle for supremacy in the Baltic. By 1660 it was recognized that Denmark and Poland had finally lost their former positions of strength. Sweden, who had done so much to bring this about, reached her greatest territorial limits and was acknowledged the most powerful state in the north. The balance of power in the Baltic had undergone its first major adjustment. But it was during these years also that Sweden showed unmistakable signs of weakness; the strain of maintaining such a position upon such slender resources was ultimately to prove too great. At the same time, Russia was moving almost imperceptibly into a new relationship with her neighbours: Sweden was harried in the Baltic provinces and Poland was quite unable to prevent Russia's encroachment westwards. Most important, this period saw the real foundation of the Prussian state. Thus it is possible to discern interesting pointers to the history of the Baltic powers in the second half of the seventeenth century.

For Sweden in 1648 the question was whether, in the face of increasing difficulties both internal and external, she could maintain the lead she had won. The Peace of Westphalia was followed in Europe by a period of unrest: there was great friction over the boundaries laid down in 1648, and in the following year Denmark was joined in alliance by the Dutch. As a result the Swedish government felt compelled to maintain for some time an army of almost full strength, a constant source of worry and expense. The granting of German territories to Sweden, in fact, resulted in added troubles which outweighed the economic advantages of these lands. She was drawn into the affairs and intrigues of the Empire, and her relationship with her German provinces may be compared with England's connexion with Hanover in the eighteenth century, leading to similar complications. Sweden now had to maintain a large and scattered empire and defend it from attack by ambitious neighbours. Denmark coveted Bremen and Verden; Brandenburg viewed with hatred Sweden's acquisition of Western Pomerania with Stettin, and Poland threatened Livonia. The length of the frontiers not only necessitated a fleet which could command the Baltic but also required well-equipped strongholds manned by efficient garrisons. The icing-up of the Baltic added to the vulnerability of Sweden's essentially maritime empire, which could only be kept together by continuous exhausting effort, and which required more than native Swedes alone for its defence. Most important, Sweden needed a large, steady income and a sound economic system; but these were to be years of increasing financial crisis.

The loss of the Prussian tolls in 1635 was a serious blow to the Swedish government, and the Regency found itself compelled to continue the policy, already pursued by Gustavus Adolphus, of selling Crown estates and revenues in return for cash. This temporarily eased the situation, but gradually more and more tenants of the Crown, who had formerly been free and independent provided they paid a regular fixed sum, were put at the mercy of the nobles, often bent exclusively on their own enrichment, and relations between the classes deteriorated. Demands that the Crown should resume its lands and revenues, and that the nobles, who were exempt from taxation, should play their part in shouldering the increased burdens, grew more and more insistent. Above all, with the loss of Crown lands, the revenue of the state from taxation declined rapidly, for it was being directed not into the state treasury but into the pockets of private individuals. On the whole the Regency was comparatively moderate in its alienation of Crown property, but the reluctance of the Estates to agree to extraordinary taxation, the inadequacy of monopolies and foreign subsidies, and the disappointing yield from the customs duties levied in Swedish Baltic ports, resulted in larger and larger areas of Crown land and other sources of revenue being given away in return for public services or sold for ready cash. At the same time Sweden's increased responsibilities demanded new and greater sources of income, and the maintenance of the armed forces was a crippling burden. If a particularly dangerous situation should result in the hiring of large numbers of mercenary troops, it would be impossible to pay them for long periods unless by war itself, and thus the army became an incentive to aggression. Under these circumstances a firm hand was needed to direct Swedish affairs, and a firm hand was just what Gustavus Adolphus's daughter failed to employ.

[19] QUEEN CHRISTINA OF SWEDEN (1644–54)

Queen Christina came of age in 1644. She had been brought up, isolated and exposed to constant flattery, destined to be the monarch of a nation whose exploits were at that time renowned throughout Europe. Her education was carefully supervised and

was, on her father's instructions, the same as that which a male
heir would have received; she had in fact a preference for mas-
culine sports and became a very skilful horsewoman. Her remarkable intellectual power and talents soon became evident;
she was fascinated alike by philosophy, the arts and sciences,
and was abreast of all contemporary thought. At the age of
twenty she was in correspondence with Descartes, the French
philosopher, and had a thorough mastery of languages, while her
court was rapidly becoming a centre of scholars, artists and men
of science. She employed eminent German and Italian musicians
and, fond of display, arranged pageants, ballets and other festivities and entertainments in the most modern style of the time.
But the great hopes which had originally been entertained of her
by the Council were to be disappointed. For all her brilliance,
Christina was unstable, vain, autocratic and selfish, with very
little common sense. She completely failed to employ her abilities
for her country's welfare, and in fact brought Sweden to the
verge of bankruptcy and social disruption. W. F. Reddaway
rightly comments: 'Six years of misgovernment by the daughter
of Gustavus Adolphus shook the foundations of the state'.[1]

At first Christina appears to have taken a keen interest in the
affairs of government and in the welfare of her subjects. Trade
and industry, especially mining, were stimulated, and in 1649 the
first school ordinance for the whole country was published. New
gymnasia were set up and foreign men of letters were encouraged
to come to Sweden. But it was not long before the round of
official duties and the petty details of administration began to
bore her, and she increasingly objected to being kept from her
intellectual and artistic pursuits. She did, however, settle the
question of the succession to the throne, appreciating the dangers
which threatened from the lack of an heir.

It had been hoped by many that she would marry her cousin
Charles Gustavus, eldest son of John Casimir, Count Palatine of
Zweibrücken, and his wife Catherine, sister of Gustavus Adolphus.
But Christina regarded the ties of marriage in general with horror

1. W. F. Reddaway, *Select Documents of European History*, Vol. II, 1492–1715,
Methuen, London (1930).

and resolutely refused to consider Charles in particular, whom she found somewhat laughable. But she was equally certain that he was the most suitable person to succeed her and determined to secure his recognition as her heir. In 1648 she successfully obtained Charles's appointment as Commander in Chief of the Swedish forces despite opposition from Oxenstierna and other leading nobles, and in the following year she proposed that he should be acknowledged as heir to the throne. The Council were violently opposed to such a suggestion but eventually Christina wrung from them a provisional acknowledgment of Charles in the event of her dying without issue. She had already secured the support of the burghers and clergy in her endeavours, and in a stormy meeting of the Riksdag in 1650 she further exploited the differences between the nobles and the commons to gain her ends. Indeed, the social unrest in the country, made worse by a series of bad harvests and the difficulties involved in disbanding the army and absorbing the troops and officers once again into civilian life, seemed to threaten civil war. The lower estates were clearly out to make trouble, demanding that the nobles should pay their share of taxation and that the Crown should resume its lands and rents. The commons feared that the whole structure of the state was being undermined. Archbishop Linaeus put it clearly when he said:

When the nobility have all the peasants subject to themselves, then the Estate of Peasants will no longer have a voice in the Diet; and when the Estate of Peasants goes under, Burghers and Clergy may easily go under too.[2]

To the aristocracy it appeared that Christina's alliance with the commons was growing stronger and that she was on the point of agreeing to their demands. The nobles finally yielded to Christina in return for her supposed abandonment of the lower estates. Thus 'by a masterpiece of unscrupulous intrigue' (Michael Roberts), she was able to extract from the nobles an unconditional recognition of Charles and his male descendants as heirs to the

2. Quoted by Michael Roberts, 'Queen Christina and the General Crisis of the Seventeenth Century', *Past and Present*, No. 22 (1962).

throne of Sweden. But, if Christina had settled the question of
the succession, nothing had been done to alleviate the financial
and social distress of the realm.

The Queen had never seriously considered giving in to the
lower estates. In fact she gave away or sold Crown lands with the
utmost recklessness, incurring widespread unpopularity and increasing the antagonism between the classes. In particular she
showered gifts of land and money on her numerous favourites,
especially Count Magnus de la Gardie, and upon her French
physician and the Spanish Ambassador. Many new peerages were
created and it has been estimated that the number of noble
families doubled in ten years. Moreover these new members of
the aristocracy, mostly persons of little significance, acquired
lands and income appropriate to their new status. It became increasingly difficult to decide what was, and what was not, the
property of the Crown, and Christina was soon forced to donate
land subject to the proviso that it had not already been given to
another. By 1654 discontent was loud and there were sporadic
rebellious outbreaks in the country. The government was unable
to pay the salaries of its officials; neither was there sufficient income to defray the expenses of the royal household.

Christina's abdication in 1654 is a baffling problem and one
which perhaps will never be fully explained. A variety of motives
probably influenced her, not the least of which was her growing
unpopularity. There was talk of civil war and, in 1651, Arnold
Messenius, son of the royal historiographer, wrote a severe attack
on the Queen and the nobles, and called on Charles Gustavus to
lead a rebellion. Both father and son were immediately executed
but Christina was only too aware that many of her subjects
looked upon her with hatred. She showed increasing signs of
weariness with the cares of government and was, no doubt, attracted by the prospect of devoting herself to culture in retirement.
Perhaps, as has been suggested, she hoped to astonish world
opinion by her action and make an even greater reputation for
herself. What we know of her vanity and capriciousness, of her
consciousness of her own greatness and her conviction that she
was unique among her contemporaries, makes this all too likely.

Almost certainly she had become a Roman Catholic before her abdication; she was surrounded at court by Catholics whom she greatly admired and was in correspondence with Descartes, who was also a Catholic and had considerable power to influence her. But under the Statute of Örebro she could not remain the monarch of Sweden and be formally received into the Catholic Church. Nevertheless both Michael Roberts and Sven Stolpe (Christina's biographer) argue convincingly that Catholicism was not the Queen's main reason although religious considerations no doubt accelerated her decision to abandon the throne. Roberts maintains that Christina, unable to marry, feared that the lack of a direct heir to the throne might result in the nobles once again becoming all-powerful, and even in the revival of an elective monarchy. Hence her determination to secure the unconditional recognition of Charles Gustavus as the next King of Sweden. Whatever the case, Christina proposed her abdication as early as 1651 but was dissuaded by a deputation of the Estates.

During the last three years of her reign, her policies became more and more wasteful and extravagant. She even contemplated an invasion of Portugal in alliance with Spain. At last, in June 1654, she relinquished the throne and Charles Gustavus was crowned Charles X on the same day. The peasantry at least were sorry to see her go. Bulstrode Whitelocke, the English Ambassador in Sweden, who was present at the Abdication Diet, wrote in his Journal in 1654:

In the last place stepped forth the Marshal of the Boors, a plain country fellow, in his clouted shoon, and all other habits answerable, as all the rest of his company were accoutred. This boor, without any congees or ceremony at all, spake to Her Majesty (and begged her to think better of her decision to forsake her people) . . .

When the boor had ended his speech, he waddled up to the Queen without any ceremony, took her by the hand and shook it heartily, and kissed it two or three times; then turning his back to her, he pulled out of his pocket a foul handkerchief and wiped the tears from his eyes.[3]

3. B. Whitelocke, *Journal of the Swedish Embassy 1653–1654*, Longmans (London, 1855).

The Queen then left Sweden for Italy, openly joining the Roman Catholic Church at Innsbruck, and finally settled in Rome where she died, poor and forgotten, in 1689.

[20] KING CHARLES X OF SWEDEN (1654–60)

Charles X, born in 1622, had been brought up carefully by his mother. He had studied at Uppsala University and had travelled widely in France, Germany and Denmark. He made his career as a professional soldier, receiving his tuition from Torstensson. In the last years of the Thirty Years' War he was Commander in Chief of the Swedish forces and thus became accustomed to authority. He developed into a firm, taciturn man, moral and magnanimous in behaviour. He treated Oxenstierna, the constant opponent of both his father and himself, with generosity, and when the old Chancellor died in 1654, he appointed his son Erik to take his place. In October of the same year Charles married Hedwig Eleonora, second daughter of the Duke of Holstein-Gottorp. This connexion seemed at the time very prudent, enlisting an ally against Denmark's pretensions in Bremen and Verden, but in the long run it was to be a real barrier to any rapprochement between the two Scandinavian powers.

In administrative affairs Charles revealed no mean skill, and it seemed that Sweden had at last found the firm ruler she needed. During his short reign he kept a vigilant eye on Crown property and always endeavoured to hear the complaints of his subjects. He endowed the University of Uppsala with a new constitution which remained in force for two hundred years, and established the first Swedish bank. He fully realized that a strong monarchy was essential to the maintenance of Sweden's position, and that steps must be taken immediately to restore social harmony and financial solvency. By this time it seemed possible that Sweden's greatness abroad might be bought with bankruptcy and the loss

of liberty at home, and Charles urged the Riksdag at Stockholm
in 1655 that the most stringent action be taken to deal with the
problem. Many of the nobles themselves realized that there must
be some resumption of Crown property, but the majority were
naturally very reluctant to yield. In the end it was agreed that
the Crown should resume all those lands donated, sold or mort-
gaged, which were specifically allocated to the maintenance of the
court, armed forces and mining industries. Elsewhere the aristocracy were to return a quarter of all lands received as gifts since
1632. This was a compromise, and Charles, unwilling to provoke
rebellion, acquiesced. Nevertheless putting even this comparatively mild measure into practice presented tremendous problems for Herman Fleming, the director of the operation, and
foreign wars and the early death of the King unfortunately prevented him from completing the work.

Charles's aggressive foreign policy: the beginning of the northern wars (1655)

From 1655 onwards Charles X's reign is a history of war, first
with Poland, and subsequently with Russia, Denmark, Brandenburg and Austria, a war which eventually led to the intervention
of the maritime powers. In fact this conflict clearly revealed the
importance of the Baltic to Europe. A number of motives impelled Charles X to embark on his expansionist foreign policy,
one of the most important being his own predilection for adventure and military glory, thus following in the footsteps of his
uncle, and hoping, no doubt, to strengthen his popularity and
power at home. He was at heart a warrior: he had served with the
Swedish army at a time when it was winning victory after victory
and it probably seemed that the solution to many a problem was
best found by the sword. In addition the domestic situation was
extremely tricky; the financial straits of the government were
constantly growing more serious, and Charles was aware of the
benefits which might be gained from a successful diversion in
foreign affairs. The state would no longer have to bear the burden
of the armed forces necessary to defend Sweden's newly won

empire, for war would enable them to live off enemy resources. Moreover, in 1651, when proposing to establish a new department of government for trade, Oxenstierna had pointed out the advantages which could result from an economic domination of the Baltic:

The rivers of the Baltic, then the noblest of the other rivers running through Sweden and her subordinate provinces – these being, besides the rivers of the old kingdom, the Neva, the Narva, the Dvina and the Oder, together with the Elbe and the Weser in Germany. Likewise the exceeding rare and precious harbours mainly in the Baltic, and in the North Sea and the Kattegat, asking only wise exploitation to benefit and avail the inhabitants of Sweden.[4]

How valuable would be the recapture of the lucrative Prussian coastline, including the greatest Baltic port, Danzig on the Vistula: such a conquest would not only link up Sweden's empire territorially, but would also, as in the time of Gustavus Adolphus, solve a great part of the country's financial problem. But there were other excuses for embarking on a new war with Poland. John Casimir, King of Poland in 1648, continued to refuse to recognize the right of the younger Vasas to the Swedish throne and a peace congress to settle the differences between the two countries had ended in total failure. More important, Poland was presenting Russia with great opportunities for expansion: Lithuania, appealing to Charles for protection, had been invaded and Sweden's Baltic provinces were menaced. In particular, the Swedish king was determined that the Prussian tolls should not fall into Russian hands.

By June 1655 the Riksdag's objections to further expenditure and their arguments concerning the strain of constant warfare were overcome, and in the following month, Charles, with fifty warships and 50,000 troops mustered from all over Sweden's Baltic empire, set out for Poland. He was undoubtedly the aggressor, for Poland was more than occupied with her own difficulties, and it was not long before he was led on to greater and greater schemes of conquest, ultimately quite unrealistic.

4. Quoted by Ingvar Andersson, op. cit.

Despite his military talents and courage, he lacked the balance
and restraint of his great predecessor.

The decline of Poland

At this time Sweden was not seriously threatened by any other
state, and Charles endeavoured by skilful diplomacy to quieten
the fears of Europe. It certainly seemed an especially opportune
moment to attack Poland, a land which was in desperate disorder. Indeed, Oscar Halecki, in his *History of Poland,*[5] comments
that one significant word –'deluge' – characterizes the series of
catastrophes which shook the state from 1648 onwards. In particular the problem of the turbulent Cossacks, situated in the region of the river Dnieper in the Ukraine, had become acute. In
their attempts to break away from Roman Catholic Poland and to
set up an independent Greek Orthodox State, their leader, Bog-
dan, in 1654 placed them under the suzerainty of Czar Alexis of
Muscovy who promised them a large measure of autonomy (a
promise which was never kept). A joint Cossack-Russian attack
on Poland ensued in the Ukraine, and Russia invaded Lithuania.
But with the intervention of Charles X, Poland and Russia, in
opposition to their common foe, made a truce in 1656 which was
to remain in force for two years. Thus Poland was, for the time,
saved from her eastern neighbour.

Internally, conditions had gone from bad to worse. The state
was torn by the quarrels and treasonable activities of the great
nobles who ruled almost independently in the provinces. From
1652 onwards the Diets were broken up with growing frequency
by the opposition of only a single vote – the famous *liberum
veto*. Thus the finances and the armed forces, which depended on
legislation of the assembly, were crippled: there was a constant
deficit and the threat of armed rebellion by the soldiers left
without pay was never absent. State officials (each with a dupli-
cate in Lithuania) were also the responsibility of the Diet and
independent of the King, who could neither dismiss them nor
create new offices in order to build up some kind of efficient

5. Dent (London, 1961).

bureaucracy. Moreover constant warfare in the 'fifties and 'six-
ties further reduced the economy and the population fell sharply.
Indeed, it is true to say that, under these circumstances, the
partition of Poland in the seventeenth century was only prevented by the mutual rivalry of her various attackers.

Charles's initial invasion of Poland met with rapid success.
Warsaw surrendered and John Casimir fled. Charles then marched south and captured Cracow, and in three months most of
western Poland was in his hands. But suspecting the Elector of
Brandenburg of plotting behind his back, Charles made a light-
ning march to the Baltic, captured Thorn and Elbing and, surrounding Frederick William in his Prussian capital, forced him
in January 1656 to sign the Treaty of Königsberg by which the
Elector was to do homage to Sweden for East Prussia and to
furnish Charles with 1,500 soldiers. Only the capture of Danzig
it seemed, was needed to complete the success of the Swedish
king.

But Charles's position was far from strong. Lack of discipline
among the Swedish forces, their plunder and outrages, led to a
national revival among the Poles which Charles was unable to
crush. John Casimir returned and in June 1656 retook Warsaw.
Moreover the Russians were invading Sweden's Baltic provinces
and the international situation had darkened. Denmark was
dangerously hostile and the attitude of both the Emperor and
the Dutch was threatening. A further treaty with the Elector,
promising him a large slice of Poland, bound him more closely to
Sweden and raised his military commitment to 4,000 men. Together they recaptured Warsaw against great odds, but Charles
was to get little further. Danzig was relieved by the Dutch, who
feared for their Baltic trade, and in November, in order to retain
the Elector's support, Sweden was forced to acknowledge
Frederick William's full sovereignty in East Prussia by the
Treaty of Labiau. During 1657 the Swedes, in alliance with Tran-
sylvania, were unable to make any permanent gains in Poland,
and Charles discovered the impossibility of holding together
such a vast, disunited state. Furthermore, Austria had taken the
field against him, and in June Denmark finally declared war.

The humiliation of Denmark

Denmark was in no state to embark on a war with the strongest military power in the north. In 1648, as a condition of acknowledging Christian IV's second son, Frederick, as king, the nobles had destroyed most of the remaining vestiges of royal power, even stipulating that Frederick should not leave the country without their permission, and Denmark found herself dominated by a selfish and incompetent oligarchy. Frederick III, learned and something of a recluse, had none of the brilliance which characterized his father, although he revealed a great deal more prudence and self-control. But he was no clear-sighted statesman and certainly was not a match for contemporaries of the stature of Charles X, John de Witt, or Oliver Cromwell. His decisions in foreign affairs were far from wise and he failed to appreciate his country's limitations. In domestic affairs he took little part, although his prestige gained a fraction from the disgrace, in the early years of his reign, of Ulfeld and Sehested, the two most prominent and capable sons-in-law of Christian IV.

The desire of both Frederick III and the majority of his subjects for revenge upon Sweden, whom they feared and hated, was very strong. Above all they were determined to recapture the provinces lost in 1645; and in 1657 the time seemed ripe to launch an attack. Charles X was fully occupied in Poland, and there appeared no serious obstacle to the capture of, at least, Bremen and Verden. But unfortunately Denmark was administratively disorganized and ill-equipped militarily or diplomatically for such a venture. A defensive alliance had indeed been made with the Dutch in 1649, but this would be no help if Denmark were the aggressor. Moreover, in 1656, Charles X had come to terms with the United Provinces and de Witt was bent on a cautious policy. Nevertheless Russia had indicated that she would support Denmark, and in 1657 Austria gave a very qualified promise of aid. Thus despite the chaotic financial situation and the poor state of the country's defences, Frederick III persuaded the Council to agree to war, and set out on an enterprise which led to ruin.

On learning of the Danish attack, Charles X, no doubt weary
of the Polish war, accomplished a remarkable march back to
Stettin. Then, meeting no resistance from the Duke of Holstein-
Gottorp, and receiving aid from Hamburg (the staunch enemy
of Denmark), he routed the Danes in Bremen and Holstein and
overran Jutland. The remnants of the Danish army fled in confusion and cowardice to the fortress of Fredricksodde, recently
built to protect the Little Belt. But all was not yet lost; it was
confidently expected that Fredricksodde would contain the
Swedes, and the Danish fleet was able to prevent the Swedish
navy from attacking the islands. Moreover Poland had made an
alliance with Denmark in August, and in the following month the
Treaty of Wehlau between Poland and Brandenburg was signed.
By this agreement Poland acknowledged the sovereignty of
Frederick William in East Prussia, and the latter, having abandoned the Swedes, offered his support to Denmark. There was
now a distinct possibility that the Swedish army might be cut
off in Jutland, besieged by the combined troops of Brandenburg,
Poland and Austria. But in October disaster overcame the Danes.
Fredricksodde fell as a result of the incompetence of the Danish
garrison, which was mainly composed of nobles and gentry, and
the subsequent extreme winter, which froze the normally rapid
currents of the Belts, far from bringing ruin to Charles, as the
Danes had originally imagined, actually assisted the Swedish
king. A triple alliance, formed in January 1658 between Brandenburg, Austria and Poland against Sweden, came too late to prevent Charles from performing one of the most remarkable exploits
in history. At the end of the month he marched his whole army
across the ice of the Little Belt to Fünen. From there, guided by
a young quarter-master, Erik Dahlberg, he set out across the
frozen Great Belt by way of the islands of Taasinge, Langeland,
Laaland and Falster, until he finally landed in Zealand. Copenhagen at his mercy, the Danes sued for peace.

The Treaty of Roskilde, 26 February 1658, annihilated Denmark's power in Scandinavia. Skåne, Blekinge and Halland were
ceded to Sweden as well as the island of Bornholm. Norway was
to hand over Trondhjem and Bohuslän, thus widening Sweden's

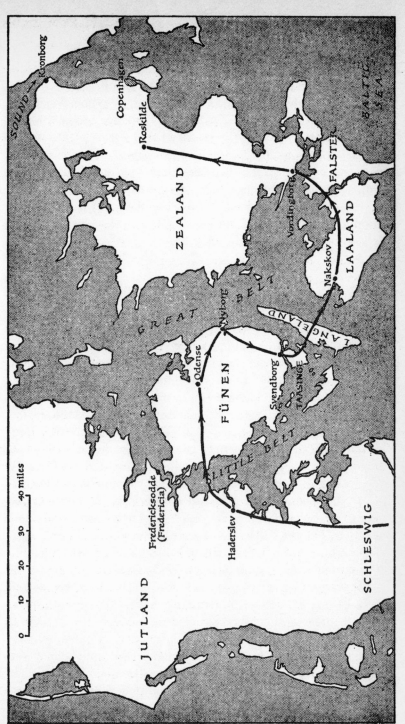

CHARLES X'S ROUTE THROUGH DENMARK, 1658

outlet to the North Sea. In addition Denmark was to renounce all
anti-Swedish alliances and to prevent all hostile warships from
passing through the Sound. Ulfeld, who had joined Charles X,
was to be restored to his estates, the demands of the Duke of
Holstein-Gottorp were to be satisfied and Frederick III was to
transfer 2,000 cavalry to the Swedish army. Peace, it seemed,
was at last assured. The Russians had been expelled from the
Baltic provinces; the maritime powers saw the advantages to be
gained from a divided control of the Sound; Charles X had
succeeded in his aim of humiliating Denmark. Finally Sweden
herself was badly in need of respite.

From the Treaty of Roskilde (1658) to the pacification
of the north (1660–1)

But the northern wars were by no means at an end. Negotiations
between Sweden and Denmark over the terms of the Treaty of
Roskilde were protracted and revealed numerous causes of dispute. Most important, Charles demanded that Denmark should
assist in closing the Sound to all foreign warships, a demand to
which Frederick III showed understandable reluctance. In fact
Charles suspected the Danes of plotting with the Dutch behind
his back and, with this menace constantly in the rear, he would
be unable in safety to proceed again to Prussia. He had clearly
begun to wish that he had completed the conquest of Denmark
and that the control of the Sound was once and for all in his own
hands. At the last moment Frederick yielded to all Charles's
demands, but the latter, visualizing a united Scandinavia, with
Denmark divided into three Swedish provinces, and all opposition
transported to Ingria, made his second attack in July 1658.

This time Charles had gone too far. The Dutch were bound by
their alliance of 1649 to come to the aid of the Danes, and such a
blatant threat to the important trade in naval stores was certain
to arouse the maritime powers in general. In Copenhagen the
Danes rallied, led by a heroic Frederick III, and Charles was
unable to bring about a swift reduction of the city. In August the
Elector Frederick William led a mixed force of Brandenburgers,

Austrians and Poles into Schleswig-Holstein and from there
invaded Jutland. But in the following month Kronborg fell to
the Swedes and Charles was at last master of the Sound. Despite
this, a Dutch fleet sailed through unscathed in October, and after
an inconclusive engagement with the Swedish fleet, relieved
Copenhagen. Meanwhile Trondhjem and Bornholm were recovered, and Skåne rebelled against its new master. Charles however
was defiant, and in May 1659 the three maritime powers joined
together in the first Hague Concert which aimed at imposing a
settlement on the basis of the Peace of Roskilde. In July, England
and the Netherlands decided to use their naval power to force
the northern powers to agree, but Mazarin this time refused to
join, not wishing to use force against Sweden, his potential ally
in opposition to the Habsburgs. On land in November a Swedish
contingent surrendered in Fünen, but Charles still remained
recalcitrant. At last, in February 1660, amidst further schemes,
including one for a winter campaign in Norway, Charles X died,
and his death removed the most serious obstacle to peace.

The three Treaties of Oliva, Copenhagen and Kardis settled
Sweden's differences with her neighbours and brought peace at
last to northern Europe. Under French mediation, the Treaty of
Oliva (near Danzig) was made in May 1660 between Sweden on
the one hand and Poland, Brandenburg and the Emperor on the
other. The dynastic feud between the two branches of the House
of Vasa was finally ended when John Casimir gave up all claim
to the Swedish throne. West Prussia remained Polish and Livonia
Swedish, and all parties recognized the sovereign power in East
Prussia of the Elector of Brandenburg. Denmark had thus been
deserted by three of her allies, and in June she too made terms
with Sweden. By the Treaty of Copenhagen, which slightly
amended the Treaty of Roskilde, all attempts to close the Baltic
to foreign warships were given up, and Denmark recovered
Trondhjem and Bornholm. Finally, in the following year, the
status quo between Russia and Sweden was restored by the
Treaty of Kardis (in Livonia).

SWEDEN'S BALTIC EMPIRE, 1660

At the end of the war therefore, Sweden, in the face of Dutch opposition, had not established an economic domination of the Baltic; she did not control the Sound, nor had she extended her influence over every inch of Baltic coastline. Despite this, she was at the height of her prestige, and her empire remained intact for the next half-century. Possessing twice as much territory as present-day Sweden, she was one of the largest states in Europe, and her military prowess was regarded with awe by contemporaries. Above all, with the acquisition of Skåne, Blekinge and Halland, Sweden had gained her long sought-after geographical unity within the Scandinavian peninsula itself and, together with the possession of Bohuslän, she had a wide outlet to the North Sea for her trade with the west.

But Sweden's weaknesses, both internal and external, far from diminishing had become more pronounced. Her empire possessed no real unity and could only be kept together by force of arms. It contained within its borders numerous different nationalities behind which were powerful neighbours poised to recover and reunite them at the first opportunity. Furthermore the danger from Russia was now greater; in Germany, Brandenburg's power was steadily advancing; in the west, Denmark was more than ever determined to recover her lost provinces. In fact the death of Charles X left the third Regency of the century to deal with an unenviably complicated situation abroad. Moreover, at home, the removal of the strong hand of the King revealed the latent constitutional controversies and social divisions. The power of the nobles over the other estates increased and the work of financial reform, initiated in 1655, came to a halt. The revenue continued to decline, while the aristocracy grew in wealth and luxury, a fact to which the numerous beautiful buildings, erected by the nobles during the middle decades of the seventeenth century, bore witness. Thus Sweden's affairs in 1660 were in a delicate condition and would require skilful handling in the years to come.

Short of actual conquest, Sweden had gained almost all she
could have wished from Denmark, her old rival for dominion in
the Baltic. Danish loss of the valuable provinces across the Sound
was a crushing blow, and the wars had left the land plundered,
the armed forces chaotic and the treasury empty. The nobles
were held responsible for all disasters and, socially isolated,
economically weakened by the recent strife, and with no adequate
leadership, they found themselves forced to yield in the face of
demands for reform. As a result, the years following the humiliations of the northern wars saw Denmark making at last a real
effort to put her house in order, while abroad she was bent on
revenge and the destruction of Sweden's supremacy.

In Poland it was almost too late for reform. The nobility refused to countenance any plans for reconstruction, and John
Casimir and his French wife were forced to abandon their schemes
when they provoked civil war. Poland continued to deteriorate,
and with the settling of the feud of the Vasas, at the Peace of
Oliva, it was Russia who henceforth presented the greatest danger to Sweden's power in the eastern Baltic. The struggle for the
Ukraine and access to the Black Sea, a contest disregarded by
western Europe, had seen the balance of power between the two
Slav powers tip decisively in Russia's favour. War had been
resumed between them in 1658, and when peace was finally made
at Andrussovo in 1667, Poland was forced to surrender Smolensk
and the whole of the Ukraine east of the Dnieper. Kiev, on the
western bank was to be ceded for two years only, but in fact it was
never returned. Henceforward, fully occupied with the Turkish
wars, Poland was unable to recover her former position. Russia
turned her attention to her more formidable enemies, Sweden in
the north, and Turkey in the south and, although far from taking
an active part in general European affairs, she gradually widened
her contacts with the west. The time was not far distant when
Russian actions would no longer pass unnoticed by the rest of
Europe.

Brandenburg-Prussia, 1640–60

The most significant development of all, during these years, took place in Brandenburg-Prussia. The Great Elector Frederick William was extremely able, thoroughly unscrupulous and determined in the national interest, and took advantage of every favourable occasion and circumstance to further his ends. The new strength of the electorate was recognized by France at the Peace of Westphalia when she assisted Brandenburg in acquiring gains quite disproportionate to the latter's part in the war. Moreover, Frederick William was acknowledged as the leading Protestant prince in Germany after his successful efforts at the conference on behalf of the Calvinists. During the northern wars his diplomacy was particularly opportunist, but for all his ambitious schemes he was unable to recover Western Pomerania and Stettin. Nevertheless his sovereignty over East Prussia was recognized and in general the electorate had shown herself for the first time to be a power to be reckoned with. But the real importance of the northern struggle for Brandenburg-Prussia lies in the use which the Great Elector made of these years to establish the basis of the future Prussian state.

From the beginning, Frederick William perceived the importance of a military force powerful enough to defend his scattered territories and to make the Electorate influential in Europe. He started by whittling down the few thousand mercenaries whom he had inherited in 1640 and who were plundering and terrorizing his lands. But his greatest obstacle lay in his weakness in the face of the local Estates, dominated in Brandenburg and Prussia by the Junker nobility and in the Rhine duchies by the towns. It was they who wielded the real power and who controlled finance. Moreover the Elector's different dominions had nothing in common, except that they happened to have been inherited by the same ruler and, engrossed with their own grievances and traditions, they refused not only to grant money to the Elector but also to assist in the defence of each other's territory. Frederick William, on the contrary, regarded his various lands as *membra unius capitis*, and his reign was to be devoted to welding them

into one state held together by the army and over which he
would have absolute power.

During the ten years after 1640 he made little headway and by
1653 he still had an army of only 1,800 men. In that year he
summoned a general Brandenburg Diet at which he suggested a
new tax to be levied alike on nobles and commons. The former
fiercely opposed this and the proposal had to be dropped, but in
return for substantial privileges, the Estates agreed to grant the
Elector a comparatively large sum payable in instalments over a
number of years. Thus Frederick was able to make a limited increase in his army; but the real military advance did not occur
until the outbreak of the northern wars in 1655. After that date
Frederick William ignored the Estates not only in Brandenburg
but also in Prussia and the Rhine duchies, and levied troops and
taxes as he needed them. In 1656, at the battle of Warsaw, the
Poles were defeated by the Swedes and the Brandenburgers and
this was the first time that troops from all parts of the Elector's
dominions had fought under one flag. By the summer of that
year, the numbers in the Elector's army had grown to 22,000, a
considerable force and one which enabled him to play an important part in the war. Later he wrote to his son:

Alliances, to be sure are good: but a force of one's own on which one
can rely, better. A ruler is treated with no consideration if he does not
have troops and means of his own. It is these, thank God! which have
made me considerable since the time that I began to have them.[6]

When peace in the north was finally signed in 1660, the Great
Elector was in a far stronger position. Heavy taxes continued to
be levied and the army was not disbanded, an efficient force of
12,000 men being retained. The struggle with the Estates was
far from over, but in Brandenburg, Prussia and Cleves alike, they
had been seriously weakened by the wars and the Elector's policy
of armed force. In addition, during these wars, a new military
institution, responsible for financing and provisioning the army,
had come into being, known as the *Generalkriegskommissariat*.

    6. Quoted by S. Fay, *The Rise of Brandenburg-Prussia to 1786*, 'Berkshire
Studies in European History', Holt, Rinehart and Winston (New York and
London, 1964).

This authority, which also remained after the war, eventually destroyed the control of the Estates over finance and administration, and endowed the state with a central organ of government directly responsible to the Elector. In short, the northern wars had provided the opportunities: Frederick William transformed them into advantages.

Principal Events, 1648 – 60

SWEDEN AND THE NORTHERN WARS

1650

Meeting of the Swedish Riksdag. Charles Gustavus acknowledged heir to throne

1654

June. Abdication of Queen Christina. Accession of Charles X

1655

Riksdag agrees to limited resumption of Crown lands. Outbreak of northern wars. Charles X drives John Casimir out of Poland

1656

January. Treaty of Königsberg binds the Elector of Brandenburg to Sweden

November. Treaty of Labiau: Sweden recognizes full sovereignty of Great Elector over East Prussia

POLAND AND RUSSIA

1654

Dnieper Cossacks acknowledge Czar Alexis as overlord. Russo-Cossack attack on Poland

1656

Truce between Poland and Russia

1657

Denmark attacks Sweden
  Charles X routs Danes
  and overruns Jutland
September. Treaty of Wehlau
  Great Elector joins
  Poland in return for
  Polish recognition of his
  sovereignty over East
  Prussia

1658   1658
January. Charles X marches   War between Poland and
  across the ice to   Russia resumed
  Copenhagen
26 February. Treaty of
  Roskilde between
  Denmark and Sweden
July. Charles X once more
  makes war against
  Denmark
October. Dutch relieve
  Copenhagen

1659
May. Maritime powers
  combine to bring about
  peace

1660
February. Death of Charles X

1660–61
Pacification of the north: the
  Treaties of Oliva,
  Copenhagen and Kardis

                                            1667
                                    Treaty of Andrussovo
                                      between Poland and
                                      Russia

Further Reading

SVEN STOLPE, *Christina of Sweden*. Burns & Oates (London, 1966).

E. HAUMANT, *La Guerre du Nord et la Paix d'Oliva, 1655–1660*. (Paris, 1893).

MICHAEL ROBERTS, 'The Abdication of Queen Christina'. *History Today* (1954).

MICHAEL ROBERTS, 'Queen Christina and the General Crisis of the Seventeenth Century.' *Past and Present*, No. 22 (1962).

See also pages 44–5.

PART V
Challenges to Sweden at Home and Abroad

A study of Baltic rivalries during the seventeenth century accustoms the historian to dynamic personalities and events. The two northern wars were no exception to this pattern. The first of these has been discussed, and the second, as will be seen below, was the climax of the whole history of the struggle for supremacy in the Baltic. In contrast, the period in between, lasting approximately thirty years, seems to lack the element of drama. International relations, both as conducted between the Baltic powers themselves, and between the northern states and the rest of Europe, were extremely complicated and often tortuous. Moreover, great personalities, comparable to those who had arrested the attention of Europe in the past, and who would do so in the near future, were on the whole absent during the three decades following 1660. In fact the true interest of these years lies in the internal developments of the Baltic nations; these developments were often remarkable and resulted in a readjustment of the relative strength of the states by the end of the century. Even so it is soon evident that drama is not wholly lacking. It was during this period that Sweden was divested, albeit temporarily, of her German provinces and Skåne, and stood forth briefly in all her weakness, thus undoing much of the work of Gustavus Adolphus and Charles X. Moreover the major part in this dismemberment was taken by Brandenburg-Prussia, the youngest recruit to the band of Sweden's adversaries.

In 1660 Sweden faced the prospect of a long period of Regency
government as Charles XI was only four years old. In his will,
Charles X had stipulated that the government should be in the
hands of the Queen Mother and the five chief officers of state,
and he no doubt hoped that by appointing his brother, Adolphus
John, as war minister, and Herman Fleming as finance minister,
he had done something to safeguard the interests of the realm
and the monarchy against the ambitions of the aristocracy. But
Adolphus John was detested by the nobility, and Herman Fleming
was in charge of the hated programme of 'Reduction' (the resumption of Crown lands). Thus it was not long before the nobles had
persuaded the other estates to declare Charles's will invalid, and
had replaced the two offending members of the Regency with
others more in accordance with their own views. Henceforth the
three most prominent members of the government were Peter
Brahe, the Steward, Gustav Bonde, the Treasurer, and Magnus
Gabriel de la Gardie, the Chancellor. The latter soon acquired a
dominant position in the government but, although an attractive
personality, well-read, and a great orator and patron of the arts,
he was, unfortunately, no Oxenstierna. Often lazy, he had no
true sense of responsibility and, extravagant in his private life,
he failed to appreciate the necessity of economy in public affairs.

The first years of Regency government were not altogether
lacking in merit: trade was encouraged; the navy was not
neglected, and in 1668 the University of Lund was founded which
was soon to play an important part in assimilating the Scanian
provinces into the Swedish way of life. But in general the internal
situation deteriorated under a mediocre government increasingly
characterized by greed and the neglect of affairs. As the years
passed the financial situation became ever more chaotic and the
national debt a greater burden. The old problems of settling the
armed forces once again into civilian life, of rewarding services
rendered in war, and of maintaining the expensive defensive

system in the Baltic provinces and in Germany, severely taxed the powers of the Regency. Discontent between the classes increased; military unpreparedness became more and more marked and in the face of noble opposition the policy of 'Reduction' was abandoned. In fact further lands were disposed of. Gustav Bonde, at least, endeavoured until his death in 1667 to bring about some improvement in the finances of the state, but he was constantly fighting against La Gardie at the head of an oligarchy animated by self-interest and with little thought of sacrifice for the common good.

Swedish foreign policy during these years was mainly in the hands of La Gardie who followed a vacillating course depending on which view happened to predominate in the Council. Basically the government wanted to maintain peace and at the same time keep Denmark isolated, but it was soon perceived that 'Reduction' at home might be avoided if large subsidies could be extracted from foreign powers as the price of a Swedish alliance. The consequences of such a policy were not, however, so clearly thought out: whether or not it might involve Sweden in war, and how far the government dare go in such negotiations. As a result, the Regency, lacking resolute leadership and militarily and financially unprepared, worked from a position of weakness, and ultimately brought disaster upon itself and upon Sweden.

In 1668, England, Sweden and the United Provinces formed the Triple Alliance against the ambitions of Louis XIV. The French king was nevertheless determined to crush the Dutch and in 1672 he launched another attack on them, having first skilfully detached their allies England and Sweden. In a treaty with the latter in 1672, France agreed to pay large subsidies and to guarantee the position of the Duke of Holstein-Gottorp. In return Sweden promised to keep an army in Germany to help France in that region if the need arose. The possibility that the need might indeed arise in a very short time seemed to have escaped the Swedes, who now had a supply of ready cash and a standing army maintained at French expense. But in 1674, in the face of a growing coalition against France, Sweden was forced to fulfil her obligations. Louis XIV threatened to withdraw the subsidies, and at last the Swedish army, bereft of supplies, crossed from Swedish Pomerania into Brandenburg. Sweden now found herself at war with the Elector Frederick William, an ally of the Dutch, and before long she had to face not only the Dutch themselves but also Denmark, bent on revenge. All La Gardie's desperate efforts to extricate Sweden from this position were in vain, and only served to exhibit the impotence of Swedish diplomacy. In the subsequent war, Sweden suffered serious reverses at the hands of powers she had been accustomed to dominate; for, since 1660, while Sweden had become weaker, Denmark and Brandenburg had grown stronger.

[23] RECONSTRUCTION IN DENMARK

The disasters of the northern wars were followed by a constitutional revolution in Denmark which freed both the King and the nation from the power of the nobles. The Danish aristocracy, with unlimited services from the peasants and freedom from taxation not only for themselves but also in large measure for their tenants, with complete domination of both local and central government, had been revealed in all their incompetence and selfishness by the humiliations suffered at the hands of Charles X. Moreover, while the nobles were incurring charges of cowardice and ineptitude, Frederick III and the burghers of Copenhagen showed leadership and courage in defence of the capital. The point had at last been reached when the lower estates would no longer tolerate a situation in which they bore all the burdens of the state and shared none of its privileges.

When the Estates (nobles, burghers, clergy) met in 1660 to discuss the financial straits of the nation, the nobles, divided and lacking strong leadership, were forced to yield in the face of the hostility both of the burghers, ably led by Hans Nansen, Mayor of Copenhagen, and of the clergy, under the equally skilful Hans Svane, Bishop of Zealand. The most capable of the nobles,

Hannibal Sehested, had been granted a royal pardon, and seeing the necessity for reform, sided with the King. While the nobility tried every means to save their privileges against demands that they should take their share of taxation and relinquish their hold over the provincial governorships, a move was made to abolish the elective monarchy and to declare Frederick III as hereditary King of Denmark. The origins of this proposal are obscure, but it was certainly supported by the court, and by Svane and Nansen. The latter persuaded the clergy and the burghers to petition for what amounted to a radical transformation of Denmark's ancient constitution. The Council and the nobility refused to discuss it, and eventually Frederick III declared that he was willing to be proclaimed as hereditary monarch without their support. The gates of Copenhagen were closed, the city militia called out, and instructions sent to the military chiefs in the provinces. But it was very soon clear that the power of the nobles was broken in the face of overwhelming opposition and in October the principle of hereditary monarchy was recognized by all three estates on condition that they should retain their privileges and that the realm should not be divided.

Hereditary monarchy did not inevitably mean absolutism, and it was generally expected that the Estates would retain some share in the government. But it was agreed that the humiliating Charter, which Frederick had been forced to sign on his accession, should be returned to him, and that the decision about the form of the new government should be left to his discretion. The Estates then dispersed with little suspicion that they would not be summoned again for nearly two centuries, or that the establishment of absolutism was so near at hand. The first step along this path was taken in January 1661, when the King was declared an 'absolute Sovereign Lord', and his advisers were soon engaged in drafting the *Kongelov*, or the King's Law. This document, which defined absolutism in the most extreme form, was completed in 1665, but was kept secret until after Frederick's death. It declared that the monarchy owed its origin to a surrender of the supreme authority to the King by the Estates, and that the only limitations on his power were that he should maintain the

Protestant religion and the indivisibility of the realm. According
to the second and the seventeenth articles:

The King has the highest and most unlimited power, for he is the
supreme head here on earth, elevated above all human laws, and he
recognizes no other judge, either in secular or spiritual matters, than
God Almighty, He can take no oath, nor make any declaration of any
kind whatsoever, either orally or written, as he, being a free and
unrestrained monarch, cannot be bound by his subjects through any
oath or obligation.[1]

Absolutism led to much needed reforms in Danish government,
both central and local, and the improvement in Denmark's internal
condition was reflected in her increased strength in international
affairs. A new administrative system, based on the Swedish
colleges, was chiefly the work of Hannibal Sehested who at the
same time rationalized local government and brought it firmly
under central control. The national debt, which had grown to
enormous proportions in the recent wars, was largely paid off by
alienations of Crown property to state creditors, and the revenue
was increased by the introduction of a new land tax.

Progress continued uninterrupted by the death of Frederick
III in 1670, and the accession of his son, Christian V, who ruled
until 1699. The new king lacked intellectual ability and had an
exaggerated opinion of his own dignity and importance, but his
warmheartedness and manly, athletic interests made him popular.
His weakness as a monarch was more than compensated for, at
least during the early years of his reign, by the abilities of his
chief minister, Peter Schumacher, later ennobled under the name
of Griffenfeld, who was one of Denmark's greatest statesmen.
He was the author of the *Kongelov* and was very influential during
the later years of Frederick III. A visit to Paris, at the time
when Louis XIV took over the government on the death of
Mazarin, had convinced him of the merits of an efficient absolute
monarchy, and in 1670 he introduced a Privy Council on the
French model, consisting of the heads of the various colleges. A
great administrator and diplomatist, Griffenfeld did much to

1. Quoted by T. K. Derry, *A Short History of Norway*, Allen and Unwin (London,
1957).

restore Denmark's power and prestige, although, almost inevitably, he began to supersede the heads of the colleges and to concentrate authority increasingly in his own hands. Under his guidance work went ahead on the drafting of a new civil law; trade and industry were encouraged and Copenhagen developed rapidly. Both the Danish fleet and the merchant navy increased in size, and this was a period of great progress in Norway under the enlightened governorship of Frederick Gyldenlöve. Indeed the Danish economy came more and more to depend on Norwegian exports of timber and fish.

During these years the Danish nobility of birth lost its political power, and simultaneously its economic privileges were undermined by the new land tax. A new high nobility no longer dependent on birth was encouraged by Griffenfeld, the son of a burgher, and it came to consist mainly of Holsteiners and other foreigners. The titles of Count and Baron, hitherto unknown in Denmark, were bestowed by the Crown on the wealthy and in 1671 a new order of merit, the *Dannebrog*, was introduced.

Thus, at home, the fifteen years of peace which followed the northern wars were put to good use by the Danes. In international affairs, Denmark's wisest course was to remain uninvolved in European conflicts in which she could never hope to exercise a dominating influence. Hannibal Sehested saw the advantages which might result from cooperation with Sweden, but during the Anglo-Dutch War of 1665–7, the two Scandinavian powers were once more on opposing sides. On the accession of Christian V, who was animated by the desire to destroy the independence of the Duke of Holstein and Sweden's power in the north, Denmark's anti-Swedish attitude became more pronounced. Griffenfeld, meanwhile, conducted the most intricate negotiations, aimed at preserving peace, raising Denmark's prestige in Europe and, if possible, securing large subsidies. He saw the dangers of a Franco-Swedish alliance, and sought above all to prevent a breach with France; the wisdom of this policy was fully vindicated in 1679. But his delicate and often obscure manoeuvres were misunderstood, and undoubtedly were influenced to a certain degree by personal interests. His schemes were ultimately nullified by the warlike ambitions of the King and his generals, and in 1676, having made enemies in every quarter, Griffenfeld was unjustly accused of treason and imprisoned for life.

With the conclusion of an alliance between Sweden and France, Denmark in 1674 had joined the coalition against Louis XIV which consisted of the Dutch, the Emperor, and the Elector of Brandenburg. But it was stipulated that the Danes should not be involved actively until another enemy attacked the allies. Thus, when Sweden invaded Brandenburg in the same year, this condition was fulfilled and, although Griffenfeld succeeded in postponing hostilities for a time, Denmark in 1675, no longer militarily inconsiderable, and strongly supported by Brandenburg, was once more at war with her Baltic rival.

[24] THE SCANIAN WAR, 1674–9

The Scanian War, as it has come to be known, during which Sweden was defeated not only in Germany, but also on the Scandinavian peninsula itself, and in the course of which she completely lost command of the sea, revealed the serious weaknesses of her Baltic empire, and shattered her prestige and the reputation, intact since the time of Gustavus Adolphus, of being the strongest military power in northern Europe. The most significant incident occurred in the summer of 1675 when the Brandenburg army defeated the numerically stronger Swedes at Fehrbellin in an engagement which was actually little more than a skirmish. None the less, it was the first military defeat of the Swedes by an inferior force since the Thirty Years' War, and it was suffered at the hands of a state hitherto quite beneath the consideration of the invincible Swedish army, despite the fact that Brandenburg-Prussia had been forcing its unwelcome attentions more and more upon the powers in recent years. News of this defeat encouraged Christian V to imprison the Duke of Holstein-Gottorp, who had promised military aid to Sweden, and to force him to hand over his fortresses to Denmark. A Danish army then marched through Mecklenburg to assist the Elector. In September 1675, Christian V and Frederick William made a treaty by which they agreed not to make peace until Denmark had regained Scania and destroyed Sweden's exemption from the Sound dues, and Brandenburg had acquired the whole of Pomerania. In the face of the combination of Denmark and the Dutch at sea, and the unexpected military strength of Brandenburg in Germany, Sweden's position began to look desperate.

Everything now rested upon whether Sweden could maintain effective command of the sea. The Swedish navy, however, was in no state to prevail against the Dutch and the Danes combined, or, it soon transpired, against Denmark alone; in 1675 it took the two flagships eight hours to weigh anchor! The Swedish Admirals, Creutz and Horn, who were in command during the decisive years of 1676 and 1677, had no experience of naval warfare, and compared most unfavourably with the Dutch Admiral Tromp and the Danish Admiral Juel. All Charles XI's efforts in the winter of 1676 to re-equip and enlarge the fleet were in vain in such a short time. Hence in May 1676 Juel captured Gotland, and off Öland, in June, the Swedish navy fled in panic before the joint Dano-Dutch fleet. Thus Sweden lost command of the Baltic and her German provinces were at the mercy of her enemies. Pomerania and Bremen and Verden were overrun, and Wismar was captured. Secure at sea, Christian V now launched an invasion of the Scanian provinces, while Gyldenlöve invaded Västergoth-land from Norway.

Complete disaster for Sweden was only prevented by the action of the young Charles XI who revealed astonishing courage and perseverence. He saved the province of Halland, and in the autumn of 1676 defeated the Danish army in Skåne at the bloody battle of Lund. During 1677 the Danes were forced to relinquish all their conquests in Skåne; but on the continent the Swedes lost everything. Another naval victory was won by the Danish fleet under Juel in July 1677 against a Swedish force of superior numbers, and the newly formed Brandenburg navy successfully blockaded Stettin and Stralsund. In November 1678 Griefswald fell, Sweden's last possession in Germany.

When not involved in mortal conflict themselves, the western powers, as was evident in 1659 and 1660, were able to exert a decisive influence on the affairs of the Baltic states. Accordingly, after the Treaty of Nymegen in 1678 had settled affairs in the west, Louis XIV took it upon himself to dictate peace in the north in the most high-handed manner. Thus Sweden had no part in the negotiations leading to the Treaty of Saint-Germain in 1679, which settled her differences with Brandenburg, and the latter was only coerced into agreement by an invasion of Cleves by French troops. Shortly afterwards Louis similarly enforced the Treaty of Fontainebleau between Sweden and Denmark. But the former, although greatly resenting her ally's behaviour, had much to be thankful for. Louis wanted a strong partner in the north, and neither the Dutch nor the Emperor were willing to see Sweden seriously weakened. As a result, despite her recent humiliations, Sweden suffered virtually no loss, while Brandenburg was forced to be satisfied with an insignificant strip of Pomerania, and Denmark gained nothing. But if the settlement of 1679 restored the territorial status quo, the balance of power in the north no longer tipped so heavily in Sweden's favour. Denmark, still no match for the Swedes on land, was not the inferior power she had been in the middle years of the century, and Brandenburg-Prussia's new strength was evident to all. Indeed, for a while, it had seemed as if Sweden's day was over, and certainly the events of 1675–9 were to be ominous portents for the future. But as yet the time was not ripe for a general dismemberment of Sweden; nor had Europe seen the last of that country's military prowess.

The inefficiency and lack of control which characterized Swedish
affairs until 1680 contrasted not only with the progress being
made in Denmark, but also, and most strikingly, with the consolidation and centralization which was under way during these
years in Brandenburg-Prussia. Despite Frederick William's contribution to international and diplomatic politics during this
period and, notwithstanding his successful military offensive
against Sweden at Fehrbellin, after which he was hailed as the
'Great Elector', his reign 1640–88 was most significant for administrative and economic growth, and for the ever-increasing
military character of the state.

Although a good beginning had been made during the northern
wars in overcoming local opposition to the Elector's policy of
centralization, the battle was by no means won. The Estates were
weakest in Brandenburg, and after an excise tax on the towns
had been introduced in 1667, the Diet gradually ceased to be
summoned. The new military and tax commissaries, the subordinate officers of the *Generalkriegskommissariat*, were in charge
of collecting the new taxes, and they gradually encroached more
and more on urban administration until the towns came directly
under the control of the new Hohenzollern bureaucracy. The
social and economic privileges of the Brandenburg nobility the
Great Elector was careful to leave intact, for, in the absence of a
middle class, it was only upon this section of the community
that Frederick William could rely to carry out his reforms.
Moreover the *Junkers* were not a leisured class as in England and
France but worked their lands personally. Therefore as time
passed, this comparatively poor class found that state service
had its rewards, and that the army provided a useful career for
their younger sons. It was a different story, however, in Prussia
where opposition to the heavy taxation, and also to recognition
of the Great Elector's sovereignty over the duchy, was very
powerful. The people of Königsberg actually appealed for help to

John Casimir, King of Poland, and began arming against the Elector. But the Estates of Prussia were extremely disunited and, with the imprisonment of Roth, the leader of the opposition, Frederick William gained the recognition of his sovereignty in East Prussia in 1663, together with considerable grants of money. But in return he had to confirm the privileges of the Estates, and the opposition was still far from silenced. In 1670, Kalkstein, the leader of the pro-Polish group of nobles was abducted and later executed, while in 1674 the resistance of Königsberg to further taxation was crushed by the billeting of troops on the citizens. Henceforth, in Prussia, as in Brandenburg, the nobility gradually entered the service of the Elector and, with the extension and development of the new system of local commissaries, the Estates eventually disappeared. In the duchies of Cleves and Mark, the Estates, after a prolonged struggle, succeeded in retaining many of their rights and privileges but, in the face of the growing strength of the electoral army, they supported Frederick William's policies and made generous financial contributions.

The new bureaucracy under the *Generalkriegskommissariat*, played, therefore, a major part in the ultimate victory over the Estates. Established originally during the northern wars, this system of administration gradually became widespread, with its officials active throughout the Elector's dominions in all matters connected with the army and taxation, and replacing the local authority of the Estates. The need for large, well-administered revenues naturally increased with the growth of the army, and the period of the Scanian War saw a rapid development in both the functions and the personnel of the *Generalkriegskommissariat*. In particular, a central military chest, the *Generalkriegskasse* was established which became before long the treasury for the whole state.

The scope of the new central authority extended to the sphere of economics, for it was recognized that greater revenue would result from more efficient exploitation of state resources. Thus trade and industry were carefully regulated, communications improved, and naval and colonial ventures financed and encouraged. Most important, the Elector's policy of immigration

came under the control of the *Generalkriegskommissariat*. As
W. F. Reddaway emphasizes, a Calvinist Elector, ruling both
Lutheran and Catholic dominions, was virtually compelled to
pursue a policy of religious toleration, and Frederick William
seized the opportunities provided by persecution elsewhere in
Europe to encourage the settlement of foreigners in Brandenburg-Prussia, thereby increasing the population and stimulating
the economy and revenue of his state. By far the most important
group of immigrants were the Huguenots, fleeing from the persecution of Louis XIV, which had culminated in 1685 in the famous
Revocation of the Edict of Nantes. The Great Elector stated in
the Edict of Potsdam of November 1685:

In view of the sympathy which we ought to, and do, feel for our
brethren of the reformed evangelical religion in France, who have
been driven by persecution to leave their homes, we . . . desire to
offer them a free and safe refuge in all our lands and possessions.[2]

It is estimated that more than 20,000 Huguenots settled in
Brandenburg in the last twenty years of the seventeenth century,
and they made a great impact on the Hohenzollern dominions,
not only by providing regiments for the army but, above all, by
reviving old, and creating new industries. They were particularly
influential in the textile trade, increasing the production of many
articles of haberdashery as well as silks, laces, velvets and stockings. Similarly the development of the copper, iron and brass
industries flourished under their guidance, and the manufacture
of candles and soap, hats, gloves and shoes, together with goods
such as watches and mirrors, owed much to the new settlers.
Many highly skilled Dutchmen also made their homes in the
Elector's dominions, and the native population learnt from them
more advanced methods of land drainage and agriculture in
general, and were taught the latest techniques in canal building.

The vigorous financial and administrative reforms undertaken
by the Great Elector during his reign, together with the stimula-
tion of the economy and a number of foreign subsidies, resulted
in a state revenue in 1688 which was three times larger than that

2. Quoted by J. White, *The Origins of Modern Europe, 1660–1789*, Murray
(London, 1964).

of 1640. But the poor and underpopulated country groaned under
a tremendous financial burden, a burden so heavy that it actually
contributed to the backwardness of the state. More than half this
revenue was devoted to the army which was far larger than that
of any other German prince and which was to make Prussia a
great power in the following century. The army first became
really formidable during the Great Elector's reign, increasing to
45,000 men during the Scanian War, and standing at 30,000 in
1688. It was thus more than twice the size it had been after the
northern wars, well-trained and efficiently administered. The
proportion of native soldiers steadily increased as did the numbers of officers who were noblemen from the electorate. Loyalty
among the latter grew stronger as the years passed and as the
state became more and more the source of all military and civil
distinctions.

Frederick William also found time to encourage higher education and German culture generally; Berlin developed both in
size and beauty. Nevertheless in some respects he failed. His
economic policy was too restrictive; his colonial and naval
enterprises died early deaths; he was unable to achieve his ends
in foreign affairs either with or without the alliance of France.
But the administrative unification and military strengthening
of his weak and scattered inheritance were remarkable achievements. They were the foundations without which Frederick
William's successors could never have built the future Prussian
state. In Europe they were labours unrecognized in the days of
Le Roi Soleil, but, in fact, as F. L. Carsten[3] points out, they out-
lasted the work of Louis XIV by many years. In the Baltic, for
the first time in the seventeenth century, Sweden's position was
challenged by another strong military power.

3. F. L. Carsten, *The Origins of Prussia*, Clarendon Press (Oxford, 1954).

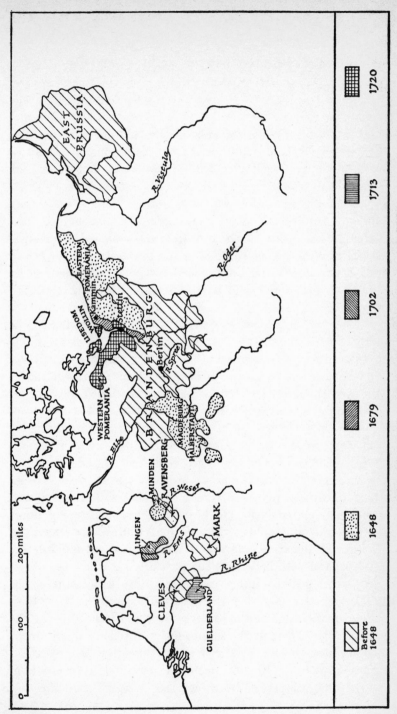

THE GROWTH OF BRANDENBURG-PRUSSIA TO 1720

Fortunately for Sweden her vulnerability did not last long. The
disasters which she had suffered during the Scanian War led to a
revolution in Swedish domestic affairs similar to that which took
place in Denmark after the northern wars, although the methods
of reform adopted by the two countries were in many ways quite
different. During the reign of Charles XI (1660–97) absolute
monarchy was established and was accompanied by radical
reforms both in the administration and in the state of the armed
forces. As a result, by 1697, Sweden's power and prestige in
Europe were restored, and it is undeniable that Charles XII's
exploits would have been impossible but for the achievements of
his father which postponed Sweden's day of reckoning in the
north. Indeed David Ogg[4] suggests that this day of reckoning
might well not have come if Charles XII had been a man of
similar character. In many ways the success of Charles XI, overshadowed though it was by the more spectacular careers of his
father and his son, justifies R. Nisbet Bain, in his history of
Scandinavia, in judging him the most important Swedish king
after Gustavus Vasa and Gustavus Adolphus.

Charles XI was not a man of great abilities. His education had
been neglected by the Regency, and ignorance contributed to his
shy and awkward manner. He was obstinate with a narrow and
often short-sighted outlook on life. But he revealed great courage
and overwhelming industry, tackling his duties with tenacity if
not with imagination. He was a man of few words, sincerely
religious, and with little time for pleasure, his chief recreations
being hunting and military exercises. In 1672 he came of age
but he still took no part in the government, and the strength of
his personality did not become evident until the time of the
Scanian War. Then, as the seriousness of Sweden's predicament
fully dawned on him, he threw himself into the task of reconstruction with wholly unexpected vigour and determination.

4. David Ogg, *Europe in the Seventeenth Century*, Black (London, 1960).

Supported by the able Johan Gyllenstierna, and in command of the Swedish army, Charles came more and more to ignore the Council of Nobles, whose incompetence and neglect were only too clear, and to take decisions himself. Thus the ground was prepared for the development of absolutism after the war.

It is unlikely that Charles XI had any preconceived schemes of constitutional reorganization, but the cause of absolutism was advanced not only by the current popularity of that system in Europe, but also by the royalist sentiments of a nation impatient with the incompetence of the former government and which had witnessed the personal courage of their sovereign in time of disaster. When the time came, Charles took control of the situation in a most remarkable manner, and step by step, a strong, financially stable, absolute monarchy was established.

In 1675 a committee had been set up to investigate Regency administration, and on its confirmation of mismanagement and self-interest, the Estates, meeting in 1680, ordered the members of the previous government to refund to the state enormous sums. This was a crippling blow to men such as the wealthy La Gardie and other aristocrats, but considerably more was in store for them. At the same meeting, the Estates assured Charles XI that he was under no obligation to consult the Council of Nobles and, when the lower nobility allied with the lower estates in support of a drastic programme of 'Reduction', the great magnates were powerless. In 1682 Charles was granted power of legislation and full control over the resumption of Crown lands: the counts and barons and other large landowners lost their large fiefs, and this was followed by a resumption of the smaller farms. All lands granted in the conquered territories were reclaimed and henceforth it was forbidden to alienate property in these areas. About eighty per cent of all alienated lands were in fact resumed during these years, and as a result the economic power of the aristocracy was broken, the Crown's finances restored to a sound footing and the peasant class saved from subjection to the nobility. The final steps towards absolutism were taken in 1693 when the Estates granted the King the power to levy extraordinary taxation as well as full control over foreign affairs.

In the same year Charles was declared an 'absolute sovereign King, responsible to no one on earth, but with power and might at his command to rule and govern the realm as a Christian monarch'. When viewed in the light of Swedish constitutional history these developments were remarkable. The Council had, since medieval times, been the main check upon the monarchy, and it had been exceptionally powerful during the middle years of the seventeenth century. Moreover, the Riksdag granted the King unlimited freedom, making no attempt to take the place of the Council as the guardian of the constitution.

Charles XI had no plans for dominating the Baltic but, determined that Sweden should not again suffer through the weakness of her armed forces, he undertook a far-reaching programme of military and naval reform. A new naval station, named Karlskrona after the King, was begun in 1680 in south-eastern Blekinge, a position which was far more at the heart of the Swedish Baltic empire than Stockholm, hitherto the chief naval depot. Karlskrona developed rapidly and became one of the finest naval bases in Europe and an important strategic centre for the operations of the Swedish fleet. The navy itself was reorganized and enlarged until by 1697 it had developed into a strong and efficient force of 43 warships. Similarly the army was strengthened and unified, and it grew to a total strength of 63,000 men, of which 25,000 manned the garrisons in the provinces. It was highly efficient, able to mobilize at very short notice. Indeed 'Charles XI bequeathed to his son perhaps the best-trained and best-equipped army ever to leave the shores of Sweden' (Michael Roberts). The principle of basing the army on the land, which had been applied in Sweden for some time, was now extended and enforced more consistently, and it remained in operation until the end of the nineteenth century. By the famous *indelnings-verk*, lands or rents were assigned (*indela* – to assign) by the Crown for upkeep of the armed forces. Officers and the men under their command lived in the same districts and provinces, and gradually, by these methods, a reliable force was once more built up. In addition, the peasants, on the suggestion of the Crown, were released from the hated duty of conscription on condition that they maintained a number of professional soldiers, often mercenaries, who were provided with farms.

Hard work brought success for Charles in other main fields of endeavour. As a result of the drastic 'Reduction' programme and the fines imposed on the members of the Regency, the revenue greatly increased and the national debt was reduced. In 1693 the King was actually able to inform the Estates that further supplies were unnecessary. Charles laboured incessantly to introduce order, economy and efficiency into the administration, and he supervised personally all departments of government. He made a large number of strenuous journeys throughout the land, inspecting Crown property and other state resources. Justice was improved, industry encouraged, and the Church was brought more firmly under royal control. In particular, Sweden's local administration was methodically developed until it became the most efficient in Europe. Taxes were generally honestly assessed and promptly collected, a factor of the utmost value during the long wars of the next reign. Intelligent administrators introduced Swedish law and religious services into Scania, and by the beginning of the eighteenth century the most remarkable progress had been made towards absorbing these provinces into the state. (Denmark was to find no supporting insurrection when she next attacked Skåne in 1709.) By 1697 the population of Sweden had increased, the towns had developed and more land was under cultivation. When Charles died in that year the authority of the Crown was supreme, and the nation was infinitely stronger and more prosperous than it had been in 1660.

But there were defects. The heavy fines and wholesale transfer of land from the nobles undoubtedly strengthened the Crown and saved the peasant class from extinction as an independent, politically active estate. Nevertheless, the 'Reduction' was often characterized by an arbitrariness which undermined the security of private ownership, and which resulted in some cases of real hardship. Modern research refutes certain of the more pathetic tales of ruin, but it is true to say that a legacy of bitterness and resentment remained with the aristocracy for a long time to come. Moreover the tradition of state service which had been maintained by the old nobility was largely lost to the state. In 1680 the Table of Ranks laid down that all posts in civil and military life should no longer be dependent on birth but upon service and merit. The growth of an adequately paid civil service was to be a permanent legacy of this reign. The new officials, who themselves amassed large estates (often buying land which the established families were forced to sell for ready cash in order to pay their fines) were closely dependent upon the monarch. Thus personal initiative tended to decline and there was less criticism of Crown policy. The ruthless programme of 'Reduction', combined with attempts to Swedify Livonia and Estonia, resulted also in the alienation of the largely German nobility of those provinces. The latter led the opposition to the resumption of Crown lands and were antagonized by attempts to prevent German students from entering the newly founded Academy of Dorpat, or from obtaining the best administrative positions. They resented the introduction of Swedish civil and religious law and the insistence upon the Swedish language for all official correspondence. Thus by the end of the reign, certain of the nobles, under the leadership of Johann Reinhold Patkul, were to be found conspiring with Sweden's rivals, negotiations which later had very serious consequences.

A revolution, although far less permanent, also took place in Swedish foreign policy after the Scanian War. The two Scandinavian powers, common sense at last overcoming ambition and rivalry, made the Treaty of Lund in 1679, the secret articles of which inaugurated a policy of cooperation. It had been recognized for some time by enlightened men on both sides that there was much to commend collaboration between the two nations, and Hannibal Sehested, in particular, had favoured such a policy. The Dutch had long exploited the differences between Denmark and Sweden, and had secured a dominant position in Baltic trade. Moreover their obvious weakness in the face of the power of Louis XIV, and the dissatisfaction of both with the settlement he imposed, gave added force to arguments put forward by Johan Gyllenstierna for a united front in the north. Consequently in 1679 the two powers agreed not to make any alliances with-

out consulting each other, and to share any benefits which might
result from a war prosecuted jointly. To seal this agreement
Charles XI was betrothed to Ulrika Eleonora, the sister of
Christian V. All seemed set fair for a drastic reorientation of
Baltic politics, the chief theme of which would no longer be the
rivalry between Denmark and Sweden. Together they would
oppose France, break the Dutch monopoly of trade, and, if
necessary, exclude the maritime powers altogether from the
Baltic Sea.

But it was only a matter of time before Denmark and Sweden
returned to traditional paths. The problem of the Duke of
Holstein, who had been restored to his former position in 1679,
was still unsettled, and in fact Sweden, during the negotiations
which led to the peace of Lund, was endeavouring to remove
some of the Duke's advisers, fearing that they were pro-Danish.
Moreover it soon became clear that in Sweden's eyes Denmark
was to remain the subordinate partner. Charles XI never ceased
to regard Christian V as his most dangerous enemy, and Christian
in his turn, was no less determined to destroy Sweden's power in
the Baltic. Both considered that the Duke of Holstein was
essential to their plans, and tension on this issue during the
following years almost led to renewed war more than once. As
a result the two powers resumed their former schemes and made
alliances aimed at isolating each other.

In 1681 Sweden, needing support in the Baltic until her own
naval power should be restored, made the treaty of the Hague
with the Dutch, which was commercially very much in the latter's
favour. In these negotiations Sweden had not consulted Denmark, and had renewed the previous Swedish-Dutch treaties of
1640 and 1645 which had a clear anti-Danish bias. As a result
Denmark allied with France in 1682, and later Christian V invaded Holstein-Gottorp, incorporating the Duke's portion of
Schleswig in the kingdom of Denmark. The situation was once
more ominous and a congress met in 1687 in an attempt to settle
the differences between the Scandinavian powers. Eventually
in 1689 by the Treaty of Altona, Denmark, fearing an attack by
Sweden, and under pressure from England and Holland, gave

way and restored to the Duke all his possessions. But the problem remained and, although in 1691 Denmark and Sweden combined temporarily to protect their trade which was threatened
by the maritime powers during the War of the League of Augsburg, antagonism flared up again over Holstein on the accession
of Charles XII. Thus, at the time of his death in 1697, Charles
XI was absorbed with the problems of Holstein-Gottorp, and his
relations with Denmark, as well as acting as mediator between
the powers of the west at the Peace of Ryswick. He certainly
did not anticipate any immediate danger from the east.

[27] POLAND IN THE SECOND HALF
OF THE SEVENTEENTH CENTURY

Poland, indeed, was now of little account in Baltic power politics,
although she was still to reveal flashes of her former strength.
Her future partition had already been foreshadowed during the
previous wars, and the election of a new king in 1669 was the
signal for renewed intrigue by foreign powers and for treasonable
activities by the gentry. Not only Sweden, Brandenburg and
Russia, but also France and Austria endeavoured to build up
parties among the nobility in the hope of exercising a decisive
influence on the election, and in the years to come, agreements
were signed between the various interested powers to maintain
'order' in Poland, by which they really meant preserving the
existing internal disorder in face of attempts at reform, and
keeping Poland weak. In 1669, however, a Polish-born noble,
Michael Wisnowieski (1669–73) was chosen, but he was incapable
and strongly influenced by the Habsburgs. It was during his
reign that Poland was forced to retreat before the Turks and to
cede to them Podolia and part of the Ukraine, valuable territories which were not returned until the Peace of Carlowitz in
1699.

During the Turkish crisis, the throne became vacant once more.

The nobles elected another Pole, John Sobieski, but this time he was a man of strong character, who in 1673 had won a brilliant victory against the Turks. The new king (1674–96), however, was no more successful than his predecessors in establishing a strong monarchy, although he understood only too well the nature of his country's weakness. He was unable to break the power of the nobles, backed up as they were by foreign countries and, in any case, his reign was dominated by the Turkish problem. In 1683 he won glorious fame by his victory over the Turks outside Vienna but, in fighting the battles of Christendom, he was unable to recover territories lost to Sweden and Russia, or to restore his sovereignty over East Prussia. The relief of Vienna, 'a feat not to be repeated by Poland until the Battle of Warsaw in 1920' (L. R. Lewitter), demonstrated clearly that the Poles were still capable of making tremendous sacrifices should the need arise. It is interesting to reflect briefly upon the consequences that might have resulted from a Polish offensive in the north and east, led by a powerful military commander, which John Sobieski undoubtedly was. The position of Sweden under Charles XI would have been even more precarious had an effective challenge come from the Poles as well as from the Danes and Brandenburgers, and Charles XII might well have had no empire to defend in the future. Fortunately for the Swedes, Sobieski was prevented from considering such a possibility and his only serious Baltic plan, made early in his reign, envisaged an alliance with Sweden and France against the Great Elector. But this project was abandoned in the face of the Turkish danger, fear of which also led him to conclude the 'eternal peace' with Russia in 1686. By this treaty, Sobieski, far from endeavouring to recover Poland's former possessions in the south and east, permanently ceded the lands lost at the Peace of Andrussovo in 1667, in return for a Russian alliance against Turkey and, while Russia's influence grew, Poland became weaker, a situation from which Peter the Great was later to benefit. In internal affairs the *liberum veto* destroyed more and more Diets; armed leagues, or 'confederations', of the nobility against the sovereign, became frequent, and Poland's decreasing military strength contrasted sharply with the growing armies of her neighbours. Thus Charles XI was safe from Poland.

[28] RUSSIA AND WESTERN EUROPE

Unfortunately for Sweden, Charles XII was to imagine he had nothing to fear from Russia. In the circumstances, this misconception, under which not only Sweden, but also the rest of Europe laboured, was reasonable. Despite tentative moves towards widening her contact with the west, and the slow progress made during the seventeenth century in strengthening the machinery of government and building up the army, Russia in 1689 was still desperately weak and backward compared with the states of western Europe. (No doubt also, the decline of Poland made Russia appear stronger than in fact she was.) Any programme of reform which aimed at breaking down the prevailing ignorance and conservatism of the Russian people, and which endeavoured to establish the Russian state on a parity with the western powers in international affairs, would need to be imposed by a man of the most extraordinary talents, a man whom the Romanov dynasty had shown no signs of producing. None of the European states recognized, nor indeed could they, in all fairness, have been expected to recognize, that in the person of Peter, the son of Czar Alexis's second wife, such a man had appeared.

When this is said, it is none the less true that the years before Peter took over the government did to some extent prepare the ground for his reforms. It was during the seventeenth century that the authority of the Czar and the Russian service state both became firmly established. The Czar's advisers came to consist more and more of a new class of nobles which developed side by side with the old boyar families, and who held their estates on condition that they performed service in the administration and the army. The other classes also had their responsibilities; the townspeople provided the revenue, and the peasants, who sank into serfdom during this century, worked the estates of the nobles and were treated little better than slaves. A national assembly, which might have checked the authority of the Czar, failed to develop, and slowly and haphazardly the central authorities (or *prikazy*) extended their activities. Thus the bureaucracy became more widespread although the government on the whole remained inefficient and unsystematic; the competence of the various offices was undefined, and the officials extremely corrupt. In the provinces the *voivodes* or military commanders, usually of noble birth, were the chief authorities, and they numbered about two hundred and fifty by the end of the century. They received a salary and remained in office for only a short time, but they were not effectively under the control of the central government. Widespread discontent and sporadic rebellions in the towns, sometimes very serious, were the result of heavy taxation and the unpopular, arbitrary methods of government officials. But, despite the obvious weaknesses, considerable progress had been made since the 'Time of Troubles'. In addition the first Russian code of laws to be printed appeared in 1649, and important strides were taken towards the creation of a larger, more efficient army. Above all, contact with the west was growing all the time.

Diplomatically Russia drew closer to western Europe in the second half of the seventeenth century and after the acquisition of the Ukraine she was increasingly influenced by the traditions and culture emanating from Poland. More important was the thriving 'German Quarter' of Moscow, mainly composed of merchants, professional men and skilled workers from the United Provinces, Scotland, England and Germany, who reflected the civilized, ingenious and largely Protestant lands they had left. They thus provided the Russians with a new standard by which to judge their own lives, and they exercised an immeasurable influence on the Russian court and upper class who were gradually to be found adopting some of the manners and customs of the west. The importance of western knowledge and skill was increasingly recognized in government circles and, throughout the century, foreign engineers, technicians, craftsmen, army

officers and doctors settled in Russia. Particularly favourable
results of this trend were to be seen in the iron and armaments
industries, and in the development of the army. Progressively
minded Russians actively encouraged this process of westernization, the most important being Ordin Nashchokin, foreign
minister to Czar Alexis. Not only did he endeavour to increase administrative efficiency and stimulate trade, but he also saw the
importance of establishing a fleet in the Baltic and breaking
Sweden's hold on the Gulf of Finland. His successor, Matvieeff,
married a Scotswoman, and their adopted daughter, Natalia
Naryshkin, considerably influenced by western customs, became
the second wife of Czar Alexis, to whom she bore the future
Peter the Great. In 1676, when Alexis died, neither Feodor
(1676–82) nor Ivan, his sons by his first wife, were mentally or
physically fit to rule and, until 1689, power fell to Sophia, the
sister of Feodor and Ivan. She soon proved herself by no means
indifferent to western ideas, and in this she was influenced by
her enlightened favourite, Prince Golitsyn.

It was during this century, moreover, that the greatest pillar
of conservatism and the strongest barrier to reform began to
crumble. Over the centuries the Russian Orthodox Church had
acquired widespread power and authority, and it came to dominate the lives of a pious and ignorant people. But during the
reign of Alexis, the Russian Partiarch, Nikon, introduced certain
reforms aimed not only at eradicating ignorance and immorality
among the clergy and laity, but also at bringing the Russian
Church into line with Greek Orthodox observance by destroying
many of the anomalies of custom and theology which had grown
up over the years. In 1667 these reforms were confirmed but they
resulted in a serious schism, or *Raskol*, within the Church. The
so-called Old Believers, who refused to accept the changes, were
expelled and harshly persecuted. Inevitably the Church was
weakened and it was thus unable to put up a successful resistance
to the progressive policies ultimately pursued by Peter the Great.

On the eve, therefore, of the Great Northern War, the Baltic equilibrium was infinitely more delicately poised than it had been in 1660, and the powers of western Europe, absorbed in the crisis over the succession to the Spanish throne, were forced to leave the northern nations to work out their own salvation. The accession of yet another minor in Sweden was to be the signal for the longest and most dramatic conflict in the struggle for Baltic supremacy.

Principal Events, 1660 – 97

THE BALTIC POWERS

1660
Regency government in
Sweden. Hereditary
monarchy established in
Denmark leading to
absolutism and reform

1667
Excise tax introduced in
Brandenburg

1674
Great Elector crushes
resistance in East Prussia.
John Sobieski elected to
Polish throne

1675
Charles XI of Sweden takes
over conduct of war

THE SCANIAN WAR

1672
Alliance between Sweden
and France

1674
Denmark allies with United
Provinces and
Brandenburg. Sweden
invades Brandenburg.

1675
Battle of Fehrbellin: Sweden
defeated by Brandenburg

1676
Sweden loses command of
Baltic. Danes invade
Scania and Västergothland
but are defeated at the
battle of Lund

1676–8
Sweden loses all her
possessions to Germany

1679
Treaty of Lund: temporary
    cooperation between
    Sweden and Denmark

1680
Swedish Riksdag authorizes
    drastic resumption of
    Crown lands. The
    beginning of absolute
    monarchy in Sweden

1683
John Sobieski's victory over
    Turks outside Vienna

1688
Death of the Great Elector

1689
Peter I takes over government
    in Russia

1697
Augustus II elected to
    Polish throne.
    Death of Charles XI of
    Sweden and accession of
    Charles XII

1679
Louis XIV imposes peace
    upon the Baltic powers:
    Treaties of Fontainebleau
    and Saint-Germain

Further Reading

MICHAEL ROBERTS, 'Charles XI'. *History* (June 1965).

L. R. LEWITTER, 'John III, Sobieski, Saviour of Vienna'. *History Today* (March and April 1962).

IAN GREY, *Peter the Great, Emperor of All Russia*, Chap. 1. Hodder (London, 1962).

See also pages 44–5.

PART VI

The Great Northern War (1)– Sweden's Brief Supremacy

The Great Northern War began in 1700 and lasted for twenty-one years. It was decisive in the struggle for Baltic supremacy, and it produced, in the words of Frans Bengtsson,

two tremendous antagonists, as different from each other – except in strength and endurance – as it was possible to be : an Olympian and a Titan.[1]

Charles XII, King of Sweden, the 'Terror of the North', met his match in Peter I, Czar of Russia. Both men were highly eccentric, and both were, above all, men of action. This conflict was in effect a remarkable duel between them, and was to bring about a radical transformation of their fortunes. Until 1707, Charles appeared irresistible. He had subdued Denmark, inflicted a shattering defeat on Russia, crushed Augustus, Elector of Saxony and King of Poland, and was apparently on the point of intervening in the great war then raging in western Europe. When it became clear that he intended to deal with Peter as he had done with Augustus, Europe heaved a sigh of relief at escaping the formidable Swedish army, and gave Peter up for lost. But the latter was to have his revenge, and when Charles set out in August 1707 on the road to Russia, a turning point had been reached in the history of the northern powers. The repercussions were to alter permanently the European balance of power.

1. F. Bengtsson, *The Life of Charles XII, King of Sweden, 1697–1718*, Macmillan (London, 1960).

[29] CHARLES XII, KING OF SWEDEN (1697–1718)

In his introduction to Bengtsson's biography of Charles XII, Eric Linklater writes:

He was indeed a remarkable man with all the attributes of a hero, some of the qualities of a saint, and the limitations of a madman,

and indeed, Charles's enigmatic character and temperament, as well as his motives and aims, have long puzzled historians; many problems remain unsolved. Unlike his great predecessor, Gustavus Adolphus, Charles XII lacked the gift of oratory, and he made no attempt to explain his actions, either to the people of Sweden, or to the diplomatists of Europe, whom he despised for their hypocrisy and double-dealing. Even his own generals suffered from his reticence and were frequently in the dark about his ultimate intentions. Documentary evidence, therefore, being almost entirely absent, the historian is forced to build up a picture from the facts available. These, together with what we know of Charles's logical mind and fundamentally virtuous outlook, suggest that he was not seeking military glory, but that he was determined to break the ring of enemies which aimed at destroying Sweden's power in the north and, above all, to punish Augustus and Peter whose treachery knew no bounds. Thus opportunities for greater victories in Denmark in 1700, and of triumphs in western Europe during the War of the Spanish Succession, which a mere adventurer seeking military renown could scarcely have resisted, were ignored by Charles, who turned away to the far more difficult military conditions of the east. In carrying out his programme, Charles's judgment was often unsound; he was excessively obstinate, and did not see the full consequences of his actions. In particular, he failed to foresee where his decision to depose Augustus from the Polish throne would lead him, a decision described by Bengtsson as the great 'lunacy' of Charles XII's life. Finally, by committing himself irrevocably to his march on Moscow, he overreached himself.

About one aspect of this extraordinary man, however, there is, on the whole, general agreement. Charles XII was an outstanding and courageous soldier, with a great gift for leadership. His energy, originality and swiftness in the field, his belief in his cause, and the devotion of the best army in Europe, brought him tremendous victories, and made him a legendary hero in the eyes of contemporaries. He was always to be seen without the fashionable wig, wearing a simple blue uniform, high boots and a gigantic sabre, never sparing himself and sharing in all the hazards of the ordinary soldier's existence. He led his troops in person, and Europe watched fascinated as success followed success for Charles XII, apparently the most fortunate of the remarkable Vasa line. But he loved war too much. His victories came too easily and he became contemptuous of his adversaries. In the end all the hardships endured by his troops, and all the sacrifices made by his country, were to be in vain.

Charles XII succeeded to the throne of Sweden in 1697 at the age of fifteen. He had been brought up in a cold, harsh, strictly moral environment, isolated from all feminine company, and carefully prepared for his future career. Charles XI, determined that his son should not be handicapped, as he had been, by lack of education, entrusted him to competent tutors. The prince revealed considerable intelligence and, with a remarkable memory, soon mastered several languages, in particular, Latin and German. He reasoned clearly and had an aptitude for mathematics; instructed in both Swedish and Roman history, he became fascinated by the science of war and all military subjects. Practical and physical training he received from his father, and he entered enthusiastically into the round of military exercises and manoeuvres which absorbed Charles XI. The latter took his son on his tours of inspection throughout the country and introduced him early to the workings of the administration. In his reserved nature, his stubbornness and his energy, Charles XII took after his father and, indeed, appears to have modelled himself consciously upon Charles XI as well as upon his great forbear, Gustavus Adolphus. But from his mother he inherited a gentle, generous side, and he developed into an altogether more complex

character than his father. In cultural matters and particularly
in architecture, he revealed superior tastes and, after his accession, court life became less austere, balls and masquerades, music
and plays, enlivening society. It is idle to speculate upon the
reasons for Charles's refusal to consider marriage, or for his
renunciation of wine, but it is clear that from an early age he
showed strength of character, maturity and ability, and the
future seemed full of promise for Sweden under such a ruler.
Nisbet Bain is probably right when he laments that Charles was
not given time, either by his subjects, or by unscrupulous foreign
powers, to develop his talents and acquire experience.

Preparations for a Regency government had been carefully
made by Charles XI, and for seven months the policy of 'Reduction' was continued at home, while abroad, the Peace of Ryswick
was successfully concluded. But since the days of Charles XI
the position of Regent was not sought after with much enthusiasm
and, when the nobility, no doubt hoping to persuade the young
monarch to restore some of their lost privileges and possessions,
invited Charles to take over the government, the five Regents
added their voices to the petition. The other estates made no
objection, and so, in November 1697, Charles XII, at the age of
fifteen and a half, became absolute master of the realm. The
nobles were, however, to be grievously disappointed. Charles
pursued his father's economic policy, and appointed Count Piper,
one of Charles XI's advisers and a member of the new aristocracy,
as his chief minister. The autocratic nature of the government
increased, the new king, according to the French minister in
Sweden, becoming even more dictatorial than his father. Certainly Charles XII crowned himself, omitted to take the coronation oath, and harshly suppressed all anti-monarchical propaganda. Government business he dealt with conscientiously, but
sometimes his youth got the better of him and, in company with
his cousin, the Duke of Holstein-Gottorp, he indulged in destruc-
tive and cruel games, often characterized by the mass decapita-
tion of animals. They went particularly wild on the occasion of
the marriage of the Duke with Charles's sister, Hedwig Sophia,
in 1698. But these days were soon over. The accession of an

inexperienced youth to the throne of Sweden, who could scarcely be expected to put up much resistance against a powerful coalition, was seen by his revengeful enemies, as a heaven-sent opportunity not to be missed.

Trouble with Denmark had cropped up immediately on Charles XII's accession. The relations of the Duke of Holstein-Gottorp with Denmark on the one hand and Sweden on the other were a constant source of danger, and Sweden's long-standing policy of protection and friendship towards the Duke, which inevitably resulted in Danish enmity, was both unnecessary and short-sighted. Towards the end of Charles XI's reign, the Duke had once more begun to build fortifications in his portion of south Schleswig, his right to do so being confirmed by the Treaties of Fontainebleau (1679) and Altona (1689). On the death of Charles XI, Danish troops entered ducal territory and destroyed the fortifications, but Charles XII soon showed that he was determined to continue his father's policy. He not only created the Duke Commander in Chief of the Swedish forces in Germany and gave him his eldest sister in marriage, but he also helped him to restore his fortifications. The situation grew increasingly tense, for the Danes were not slow to realize the implications of the situation should Charles XII die without issue, and throughout 1699 Denmark and Sweden made open preparations for war. But apart from the storm-centre of Holstein-Gottorp, the international situation in the north appeared calm. Both Augustus of Saxony and Peter of Russia had hastened to assure Sweden of their friendship, and Charles XII and his advisers remained quite unaware of the intrigues busily being pursued against them behind the scenes.

[30] THE COALITION AGAINST SWEDEN

As early as 1697, the Czar, during his 'grand embassy' to western Europe, had negotiated an alliance with the Elector Frederick III of Brandenburg (soon to be King of Prussia) which aimed at protecting them from their mutual enemies, notably Sweden. In the same year, Peter gave powerful support to Augustus II, Elector of Saxony, who was elected King of Poland in the summer. This thoroughly unscrupulous adventurer, constantly involved in schemes and intrigues, brought disaster upon Poland, and inaugurated sixty-six years of rule by kings from the House of Saxony, aptly described by Oscar Halecki as a period of 'decay'. Poland above all else needed peace, and since the Treaty of Oliva there was no genuine reason for renewing war with Sweden. But Augustus, eager for renown, and hoping to acquire Livonia, became the leader of the coalition against Sweden, into which Poland, her territory once more destined to become a battleground, was dragged against her will. In his negotiations Augustus actually promised large slices of Polish territory to his various neighbours in return for their support. Apparently he ambitiously saw himself as a Polish Louis XIV, playing a similarly dominant role in eastern Europe. As it turned out he merely completed the ruin of Poland, for during his reign all hope of recovering Livonia and East Prussia was finally lost, and the Czar of Russia established himself as the true master of that unfortunate country.

During 1698, anti-Swedish negotiations between the northern powers speeded up. The most significant move took place in August when the Czar, on his return from his tour of the west, met Augustus at Rawa in southern Poland. Peter himself, when writing the introduction to the official history of the northern war at the end of his reign, stated that at this meeting the two monarchs discussed future action which might be taken against Sweden. Augustus, in return for Russian aid against Polish rebels, was to help Peter take revenge for insults he alleged he had suffered at Swedish hands when passing through Riga (in Livonia) on his way to the west. As yet, however, the time was not ripe for anything more than exploratory conversations, for Peter had a war with Turkey on his hands, and was resolved to bring it to a successful conclusion first. But with the arrival of Patkul, the rebellious Livonian nobleman, at the court of Augustus in October 1698, Sweden's danger increased. Patkul had been forced to flee from Sweden on a charge of treason, and realizing that he would be unable to return to his beloved Livonia while it remained in Swedish hands, he set about inciting Augustus to undertake its conquest. There certainly seemed little for the Livonian aristocracy to fear from Poland or its irresponsible king. Thus Patkul revealed secret documents from Livonian nobles who were ready to acknowledge Augustus as their king, and drew up schemes for the conquest of Sweden and the partition of her several territories. Augustus should gain Livonia (in theory for Poland, but in practice as a hereditary possession of the Saxon House), Denmark would receive part of Bremen and Verden, Brandenburg was to have Swedish Pomerania, and Russia would obtain Ingria and Carelia.

Augustus was not slow in accepting these ideas and during 1699 the coalition took its final shape. A good understanding was soon reached between Augustus and his uncle, Christian V of Denmark, to whom Patkul had been sent in the spring of 1699. The accession of Frederick IV to the Danish throne in August, even more eager than Christian to strike at Sweden, did not delay proceedings, and in September he signed an offensive alliance with Augustus. The latter was to invade Livonia early in 1700, while Frederick would launch a simultaneous attack upon Sweden from Schleswig and Norway. The treaty was, however, only to be binding if the Czar acceded to it.

The original idea had been to draw in Brandenburg-Prussia, whose ambitions in the north had been only too evident in recent years. But the Elector Frederick III feared the military power of the Swedes and, even after the battle of Poltava, refused to declare war upon Charles XII. Moreover Frederick was extravagant and he depended more and more for the upkeep of his large and expensive army upon foreign subsidies. Neither Charles XII nor Peter I showed any inclination to pay for his services, whereas in the west the case was very different. Most important, Frederick had begun protracted negotiations with the Emperor aimed at securing imperial agreement to his taking a royal title. Eventually in November 1700, with the Spanish Succession War almost upon him, the Emperor reluctantly purchased Frederick's mili-

tary aid against France by granting him a subsidy and agreeing
to recognize his title as king in Prussia. Certainly Prussia's true
interests lay in the north and east, in the acquisition of Swedish
Pomerania and West Prussia, and there is little doubt that the
Great Elector would not have let such an opportunity pass. But,
as it was, Patkul's hopes were disappointed and when in July
1700 Peter sent his ambassador to Berlin, confident after the
conversations of 1697 that Frederick would react favourably to
an anti-Swedish offensive, his proposals were rejected.

In contrast, the Czar had shown himself very willing to take
part in the enterprise provided he could end the Turkish war
satisfactorily. Since 1698 he had been negotiating with Christian
of Denmark and, after his meeting with the Polish king at Rawa,
his enthusiasm to aim a blow at Sweden had increased. In
September 1699 Patkul arrived in Moscow, by chance at the same
time as a Swedish embassy hoping to renew the Treaty of Kardis,
and Peter, assuring the Swedes of his undying friendship, conducted his negotiations with Patkul under their very noses. A
memorandum, probably drawn up by Patkul, emphasized the
great political and economic benefits which would result from
Russian acquisition of the Baltic seaboard, and Peter became
more and more impatient to obtain peace with Turkey. An alliance between Russia and Denmark was at last concluded, and
the Danish ambassador took part in the negotiations between
Russia and the Saxon mission. Finally, in November 1699, a
treaty was signed between Augustus and Peter by which the
latter was to attack Ingria and Carelia not later than April 1700.
But Peter was careful to include in the agreement a clause which
stated that peace between Russia and Turkey must be concluded
first.

Russia's active participation in the coalition against Sweden was to be the deciding factor. In Peter I the Romanovs had at last produced an exceptional leader, one who was to be the founder of modern Russia and who revealed for the first time the great potentialities of the Russian land and people.

He made Russia conscious of great destiny, and ever since Europe and Asia have had to reckon with her.

comments B. H. Sumner in his admirable *Survey of Russian History*.[2] As this historian points out, Peter did not create a new form of state, but built upon the absolutism, the class structure and the laws of old Russia which had developed over the centuries. What was revolutionary was the way in which Peter, with his great ability, determination and inexhaustible energy, forced a backward and unwilling nation to accept at a killing pace the technical knowledge of the west as well as many other aspects of its civilization, in order that Russia might stand as an equal with the rest of Europe. Sumner continues:

He opened wider with sledge-hammer blows fissures which had already been spreading in the half century before 1700.

In carrying out this policy, Peter drove Russia too hard and much of his work, piecemeal and superficial, died with him. But Russia was never to be the same again. Henceforth she ranked as one of the major European powers and the isolation of the seventeenth century was at an end.

Peter was born in 1672, the son of Natalia Naryshkin, Czar Alexis's second wife. Four years later Alexis died and this was the signal for a long period of intrigue and political strife between the rival families of his two wives – the Miloslavskys and the Naryshkins. Feodor, the eldest surviving son of Mary Miloslavsky, was proclaimed Czar, but in 1682 he died childless. He left no

2. Duckworth (London, 1944).

directive as to the succession and the choice was thus between his younger brother Ivan, half-blind and practically an imbecile, and Peter, a boisterous, healthy boy, six years Ivan's junior. A group of nobles, headed by the Patriarch, proclaimed Peter as Czar, but Sophia, Ivan's able elder sister, aided by many of the Streltsi, a hereditary, privileged and reactionary body, which made up the palace guard and garrison of Moscow, had other plans. Fearing the exclusion of herself and her family from all effective power, she stirred up the Streltsi against the Naryshkins and, believing rumours that the latter were plotting to kill Ivan and seize power, the Streltsi marched on the Kremlin, demanding to see the royal children. Terrible bloodshed ensued; Matvieeff and other supporters of the Naryshkin family were massacred by the Streltsi before Peter's eyes, a scene which he never forgot. Such violence and instability in his early childhood were unlikely to aid Peter's development into a responsible individual, and no doubt explain much of his later behaviour. Ivan and Peter were now proclaimed joint Czars, with Sophia as Regent but, while the latter lived with Ivan in the splendour of the Kremlin, Peter and his mother retired for longer and longer periods to the village of Preobrazhenskoe, just outside Moscow and near the 'German Quarter'. As a result the scanty, formal instruction which Peter had so far received, came to an end; his secondary education was to be totally different from his primary, and unlike that of any previous Russian czar.

At Preobrazhenskoe Peter indulged in elaborate military games and devoted much of his time to learning practical trades such as stonemasonry, carpentry, printing, and, later, even dentistry. In his increasing dexterity in the practical skills Peter took great pride and he was for ever showing off his work-worn hands. (He was eventually to boast that he was the master of fifteen trades.) For the technical knowledge needed for his various pursuits he turned to the 'German Quarter', and from a Dutch merchant named Timmerman, he began to learn geometry and arithmetic, and studied methods of fortification and the science of ballistics. He had a keen and receptive mind, was insatiably curious and always eager to experiment. Gradually, from among the sons of the

local nobility and the peasantry, and from the large staff of royal
servants, he built up two regiments of three hundred men each,
later to be the nucleus of his new Russian army. Fortresses and
barracks, offices and stables were constructed, and complicated
military exercises were staged for which he made full use of the
state arsenal. When he was almost seventeen, the accidental discovery of an old English boat in a storehouse awakened his passion for the sea, and once again he called upon his foreign friends
to instruct him in sailing and ship-design. Throughout this period
of freedom, Peter followed his own inclinations, taking no part in
court ceremonial and showing no interest in his new bride whom,
on his mother's insistence, he dutifully married early in 1689.
Within three months he had parted from her, although in the
following year she bore him a son, the ill-fated Alexis.

It was in 1689 that Sophia fell from power. Her campaigns in
the Crimea against the Turks had been expensive failures and
rumour was increasing that she intended to seize the crown.
Tension grew between her supporters and those of Peter, now of
an age to rule, and when in August a report circulated that the
Streltsi were on their way to murder him, Peter fled in panic to
the strongly fortified monastery of Troitsa, a place of special holi-
ness, where his safety was assured. Here his family, his play-
regiments and the Patriarch rallied to him and, on Peter's
summons, the foreign officers and most of the Streltsi joined him
also. Sophia found herself virtually deserted and three weeks later
she was banished to a nunnery. Peter now returned to Moscow,
but it was to be another five years before he actually took over the
government. In fact he became even more absorbed in his games
of 'Mars and Neptune', as he termed them. To the dismay of his
subjects he was constantly to be seen in the 'German Quarter' in
company with his new friends, Gordon, an intelligent Scot, and
Lefort, a pleasure-loving, hard-drinking Swiss, from whom he
acquired technical instruction and some knowledge of the life of
western Europe. Meanwhile his regiments grew in size and efficiency; military expeditions and manoeuvres increased and Peter
experimented with guns and fireworks, and new techniques of
every kind. Above all, he sought to master the art of designing

and constructing ships. In 1693 and 1694 he satisfied his desire
to see the sea and real ships when he made the long journey to
Archangel where he eagerly examined everything, and whence
he returned fired with enthusiasm and determined to create a
navy. On the death of his mother in 1694, Peter at last assumed
the responsibilities of government, and in the following year he
was to gain his first taste of warfare at the siege of the Turkish
fortress of Azof.

The Czar was now twenty-two, almost a giant in height and
physique, revealing already many of the characteristics which
became familiar in later years. He was a man of great contrasts,
with a violent, unstable temperament and a tendency to epilepsy.
At times he became a barbarian, cruel, vicious, cowardly and
often coarse in the extreme. He indulged in licentious, drunken
orgies and in blasphemous mockery of the Church. He treated
people as tools to be used for his purposes and, on occasions, revealed a total disregard for human life. But he was also shrewd
and highly intelligent, and could show deep affection towards his
friends. His energy was tremendous: he rushed headlong from
place to place, from project to project, adopting new ideas and
schemes, planning far-seeing reforms, and all this, not for his own
glorification, but for the good of Russia, to which he devoted all
his strength.

Just as, in the north, Sweden barred Russia from the Baltic
Sea, so, in the south, Turkey prevented Russian access to the
Black Sea. In 1686, in return for Poland's permanent cession of
Kiev, Russia had been drawn into the European coalition against
the Turks, and in 1695 an attack was launched on Azof. Situated
about ten miles from the mouth of the river Don, this fortress, if
taken, would give Russia an outlet to the sea and valuable harbours; the enterprise failed because the Russians could not prevent Turkish reinforcements reaching Azof by sea. Peter, therefore, resolved to create a fleet to blockade Azof, and at Voronezh,
on the upper waters of the Don, near rich timber resources, this
formidable task was undertaken. The Russian people had no
interest in, or experience of, the sea and the shortage of skilled
workmen was acute. Moreover, not only had the design of the

ships to be chosen, but the shipyards in which to build them had
to be constructed, and the officers and crews trained from scratch.
Carpenters were brought from Archangel and shipwrights from
abroad. From Holland came a galley to serve as a model for the
fleet, and thousands of peasants, many of whom died of sickness
or deserted, were forced into the unfamiliar work of shipbuilding.
Everything had to be accomplished with the utmost speed during
the winter of 1695–6, and Peter, who directed the whole operation, worked day and night. In the middle of these preparations
(January 1696) came the death of Czar Ivan: Peter was now
indisputably master of Russia. At last a small fleet was ready,
the nucleus, it was hoped, of a powerful Black Sea navy, and in
the summer of 1696, it successfully blockaded Azof. The port,
deprived of supplies, surrendered in the face of the Russian
artillery (Peter himself serving as a bombardier), and its fall was
hailed in Russia as a great victory. Peter's enthusiasm for a navy
and for more knowledge from the west was further aroused, and
he sent a group of young nobles abroad to learn the latest naval
techniques. Moreover, in the first half of 1697, fifty foreign shipwrights arrived in Moscow, and work on the new navy, the cost
of which was spread equally over the whole nation, went relent-
lessly ahead. It was in March of that year that Peter, to the horror
of his people, took the unprecedented step of departing from
Russia in order to see the countries of the west for himself.

The 'grand embassy' of 1697–8, consisting of some two hundred and fifty persons, was headed by Lefort, with Peter travel-
ling as a volunteer sailor under the name of Peter Mikhailov, an
incognito to which he scarcely adhered. The formal object of the
mission was to persuade the nations of Europe to join with Russia
in a great crusade against the Turks, but this scheme met with
scant sympathy. The western alliance, headed by England and
the United Provinces, was too concerned with the prospect of
renewed war with France, and could not afford to see the resources of the Empire employed once more against Turkey. It
no doubt also occurred to these powers that Turkey might be
prevented from rendering possible assistance to France, with
whom she was on friendly terms, if the Russo-Turkish conflict

were renewed. But Peter was well aware that he had no chance
against Turkey if he stood alone, and it was from this time onwards that Russian policy took on a decidedly anti-Swedish bias,
while an honourable peace was sought with the Turks. The other
purposes of the Czar's embassy, however, bore much greater
fruit. Macaulay was right when he commented:

His journey is an epoch in the history, not only of his own country,
but of ours, and of the world.

In the United Provinces and England, the two countries Peter
most wished to visit, he observed at first hand western techniques
of shipbuilding, navigation, industry, commerce and administration, and in general examined every aspect of the power and
thriving material prosperity which were so evident in these states
and so lacking in Russia. The Czar himself worked in the shipyards of Amsterdam, as well as in the royal dockyards at Dept-
ford, where he was lodged in John Evelyn's house (which he and
his party wantonly damaged). He remained in England for four
months, visiting the docks, Woolwich arsenal, the Tower, the
Houses of Parliament and the Mint. In the main he was interested
only in western knowledge which had a strictly utilitarian value,
and he made little or no effort to understand the political and
cultural background and institutions of these nations. But the
contrast between the Anglican Church and the Russian Orthodox
Church fascinated him, and he had deep discussions with Bishop
Burnet, the author of *History of My Own Times*, whose original
highly favourable impression of the Czar underwent a rapid
change on learning of Peter's later massacre of the Streltsi. At
last, having joyfully accepted William III's generous gift, the
new yacht *Royal Transport*, the Czar began his return journey.
In the eighteen months which he spent in the west he had absorbed
much useful knowledge, as well as having purchased quantities
of military and naval supplies, and recruited some 750 sailors,
shipwrights, engineers and other skilled craftsmen, to his service.
Russia was soon to feel the full effects of her ruler's unorthodox
education.

News of a serious revolt by the Streltsi forced Peter to abandon

his plan of spending some time in Venice on his way home. The
rising was in fact put down by foreign mercenaries in Russian
service before his return to Moscow in August 1698, but he had
now made up his mind to exterminate the only body which
could effectively oppose his plans, and which had terrorized him
as a child. He was himself present at the subsequent terrible
interrogations and torture, and during the next two years about
1,200 men were hanged, broken on the wheel or beheaded, while
others were banished to Siberia, and the remaining regiments
disbanded. Although nothing could be proved against Sophia,
Peter forced her to take the veil and considerably reinforced the
guard which he kept on her. With this dreadful bloodbath a new
era had begun.

Only the day after his return from the west, Peter personally
hacked off the beards of some of his courtiers. Decrees ordering
shaving and western dress soon followed, for the Czar was bent
on eradicating the impression of outlandishness which westerners
received from the beards, flowing robes and high pointed hats
normally worn by Russians. In 1699, A. A. Matvieev was sent
to the United Provinces as Russia's first permanent diplomatic
representative abroad. In the same year local government was
made more efficient, giving the burghers, instead of the voivodes,
control over the towns as well as over many of the taxes, and a
central office to supervise the new municipal bodies was set up in
Moscow. The merchants were also instructed to form companies
for trading; tobacco was henceforth actively encouraged, providing a valuable source of income; and under Peter's direction many
new iron foundries were established. In 1700 a beginning was
made on the long overdue reform of the coinage, and it was also
decreed that the new year should begin in January, not September, and that years should no longer be reckoned from the Creation. A lucrative stamp duty was introduced, a commission set
up to examine the legal code, and preliminary moves made towards educational reform. The navy, which was slowly taking
shape in the south, took up much of the Czar's time and, in 1699,
an impressive fleet of 12 warships was launched at Azof. Already,
therefore, a deliberate policy of westernization was being pursued,

and the Russian people, forced along a harsh, unfamiliar road, were rapidly discovering the force of Peter's will.

The Czar was now anxious to conclude the war with Turkey and concentrate all his resources on the new enterprise in the Baltic. The Emperor, Poland and Venice had already made peace with Turkey at Carlowitz in 1699, but Russia's interests had been ignored, a fact which increased Peter's determination to make his country count in Europe. At first he pitched his demands high but the Turks adamantly refused to concede to Russia freedom of navigation of the Black Sea and the Straits. Eager to begin hostilities in the north, Peter was forced to moderate his instructions, and finally, in August 1700, he received word from his envoys that peace had been signed, Russia gaining Azof, but no more. Immediately he declared war on Sweden despite the fact that his military preparations were scarcely adequate; he had not begun creating an army until the previous November, although in three months he raised twenty-nine new regiments. But they consisted mainly of domestic serfs and surplus monastic servants who remained raw and inexperienced, certainly no match for the Swedes, in spite of every effort by foreign officers employing up to date methods. Indeed Peter gravely underestimated his opponents. Moreover, when he embarked on war, he had not received the news that Denmark had already dropped out of the coalition.

[32] THE OUTBREAK OF THE GREAT NORTHERN WAR: CHARLES CRUSHES THE COALITION

As it happened, the Great Northern war had begun disastrously for the allies, at first so confident of victory. In March 1700 Charles XII received the disturbing information that Augustus and the Saxons had attacked Riga. Shortly afterwards Frederick IV, calculating that his fleet was strong enough to protect Zea-

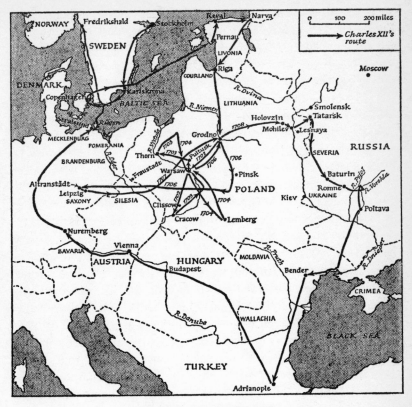

CHARLES XII IN EUROPE

land, invaded Holstein with most of his army. Unfortunately, however, for Danish plans, William III, anxious to avoid a northern conflict on the eve of the Spanish Succession War, and guarantor, with Sweden, of the Treaty of Altona, which had settled the position of the Duke of Holstein, dispatched a combined Anglo-Dutch fleet to the Baltic, and it passed unmolested through the Sound in June. Charles, energetically directing military and naval preparations, then persuaded his unwilling admiral to send all but the largest vessels in the Swedish fleet through the dangerous eastern channel of the Sound (thus avoiding the Danish navy) to join up with the Anglo-Dutch squadron. This operation successfully completed, Charles, protected by three fleets, led his army across to Zealand and threatened Copenhagen. Frederick IV rapidly abandoned his plans, and on 8 August signed the Peace of Traventhal with the Duke of Holstein, by which the King satisfied all the Duke's demands and undertook not to aid the enemies of Sweden. Charles received this news at the very moment when he was advancing on Copenhagen and, as the maritime powers made it clear not only that their task was at the end, but also that they would oppose a Swedish offensive, he bitterly resigned himself to the situation. In any case, events in the east demanded all his attention. In May he had learnt that Augustus had been repulsed from Riga, but Charles was fully aware that another Saxon attack would soon follow. Then came word that hordes of Russians were pouring into Ingria, and thus on 1 October 1700, the Swedish fleet set sail for Pernau, a port conveniently situated between the enemies. On arrival Charles discovered that the Russian siege of Narva was the more serious problem. He decided that Riga could wait and, after accomplishing a long, hard march at remarkable speed, he pitched his camp on 19 November seven miles from the besieged fortress.

In fact, Charles, only eighteen years old, was taking an enormous risk. Having forced-marched his army of only 10,000 men through appalling conditions, often knee-deep in mud and slush, and with only sufficient food for four days (although the march took seven), he faced an enemy which outnumbered his own force by four to one. In the circumstances the Swedes were fortunate to escape defeat, and the rapidity and totality of Charles's triumph was astonishing. The Russians, having received greatly exaggerated reports of Swedish strength, lacked confidence. They had little effective artillery, and the Czar himself had ignominiously left camp only eight hours before the Swedish attack, bequeathing the command to an unwilling, elderly, Belgian officer, the Duc de Croy. Later Peter was to admit that he had entered the war completely unprepared, and unaware of the strength and experience of the Swedish veterans. Thus, on 20 November 1700, the Swedes routed their panic-stricken opponents, the majority of whom, confused and blinded by driving snow, took refuge in flight. Many of the foreign officers were massacred by the men they had trained, and only two guards regiments effectively stood their ground. Soldiers in their thousands were killed, several Russian generals and colonels and many other officers were captured, and all the Russian artillery and stores were taken by the Swedes, who themselves lost well under 2,000 officers and men. But not only did the Czar sustain heavy material casualties; he also lost what little prestige he had among the nations of Europe. In contrast, Charles, in the words of his biographer, Bengtsson:

From that hour . . . ranked among the heroes . . .,

and upon him was bestowed,

renown, world-wide renown such as has perhaps never been bestowed on anyone so instantaneously, so completely; certainly never upon one of his age.

Unfortunately, however, the ease of his victory meant that he henceforth looked with scorn on his Russian adversary.

The Swedish king was now eagerly sought after as an ally by diplomats from both opposing camps in the struggle for the Spanish inheritance, but all inducements to Charles to abandon the northern conflict were in vain. His ministers also, led by the Chancellor, saw him playing an important role in Europe, mediating between the powers of the west, and winning even greater prestige for himself and his country. But Charles would have none of it. He aimed, quite naturally, at crushing Augustus and Peter once and for all, but as he could not deal with them simultaneously, the question was which of them was the more dangerous, and therefore to be tackled first.

In either case, winter quarters after Narva were essential as the Swedish troops, suffering from the severe weather and increasing sickness, were becoming depleted. Charles thus moved to Livonia and in the following May began receiving welcome reinforcements from home. In June 1701, with some 18,000 men, he made a daring crossing of the river Dvina in the face of enemy guns, and smashed a combined Russo-Saxon force which numbered about 28,000. Riga was thus saved, the Saxons dispersed,

and the Duchy of Courland duly occupied. Now was the moment
to invade Russia, and there is evidence that Charles originally
planned to do so. Unfortunately he changed his mind and turned
against Augustus whom he was to pursue through Poland and
Saxony for the next six years. Peter, meanwhile, was given what
he needed above all else – time, time to restore his army and his
morale, time to establish himself in the Baltic provinces. Charles's
decision, as it turned out, was a serious miscalculation, but one
for which, in fairness to him, there seemed very strong reasons
at the time. Militarily the Saxons were generally regarded as
infinitely more formidable than the Russians, and Charles felt
unable to embark on a major campaign in Russia with such a
force in his rear. Moreover the Elector must have appeared the
greater of the two scoundrels, for, in contrast to Russia and
Denmark, Saxony-Poland had no genuine cause for enmity
towards Sweden, and yet it was Augustus who had been the
central figure in the anti-Swedish coalition. Thus Charles XII
determined to punish him but, in doing so, he conceived the
unhappy scheme of deposing Augustus from the Polish throne.
This was another mistake, for Augustus was certain to resist to the
bitter end. Moreover it involved Charles in a far-reaching military
enterprise, and one which was impractical politically. But as
time passed, it became increasingly plain that Charles XII's view
of international politics, egoistic, utterly personal and uncom-
promising, was hardly sane.

Having therefore secured Livonia, Charles, in January 1702,
set out for Warsaw which he took in May; in July, at Clissow, he
overwhelmed a vastly superior force of Saxons and Poles. The
Swedish cavalry brilliantly distinguished themselves at this
battle, but Charles suffered a personal loss when his brother-in-
law, the Duke of Holstein-Gottorp, was killed. In the same month
Cracow was captured, and in April 1703 the Saxons sustained
another defeat at Pultusk. In October Charles captured Thorn,
and thus held the key to the important basin of the river Vistula.
Gradually he built up a party among the Polish nobility and, in
January 1704, they were prevailed upon to form a 'confederation'
and to renounce allegiance to Augustus. After some difficulty

in finding a successor, Charles finally selected a respectable but colourless Polish noble, Stanislas Leszczynski, and considerable bribes, together with the presence of Swedish troops, brought about his election by a small minority of the nobles in July 1704. Charles then departed south-eastwards intending to smash the Saxons and Russians who were gathering in the region of Lemberg. Greatly daring, he stormed and took the fortress with only a handful of dragoons but, meanwhile, Augustus had slipped northwards and regained Warsaw. Charles returned swiftly and drove the Saxons over the Silesian border into Saxony. Eventually, in September 1705, Stanislas Leszczynski was crowned with great splendour, Charles having provided him with the necessary regalia. A treaty with the Polish kingdom followed as well as trade agreements highly advantageous to the Swedes. But Charles's hope of establishing a strong and friendly Poland under its new king was to be in vain. Stanislas, far from being a help, was altogether too weak to maintain himself in such an unstable position, and was constantly in need of assistance. At the time, however, Charles appeared to have met with uninterrupted success. His victories had been won with ease, nearly always against superior odds, and it would have been remarkable had he not despised opponents who so often took flight at the first opportunity. But while Charles remained in Poland, he did nothing to build up Sweden's strength in the Baltic provinces where, in the face of an increasing Russian offensive, the situation was becoming critical.

Far from being deterred by the disaster of Narva, Peter had been stimulated by the defeat, and he threw himself with frenzied speed into the task of reconstructing his defences. Russia lay open to Charles, and Peter expected a devastating attack at any moment. Bengtsson comments:

Seldom can a hysterical urge for self-preservation have been so powerful a source of energy as in Peter's case in the period between Narva and Poltava.

Almost immediately the troops which had scattered at Narva were reformed into a new army, soon to number about 34,000

men, and, hampered by insufficient metal to replace his lost
artillery, Peter ordered the bells from churches and monasteries
to be cast into cannon. New iron foundries, armament and cloth
factories were established, and munitions and supplies were produced in increasing quantities. The army was trained by the
latest methods and re-equipped with modern weapons which in-
corporated some new inventions. In particular, the cavalry was
re-armed with pistols, muskets and broadswords, while the
development of a new lighter gun increased the mobility of the
artillery. Great emphasis was placed on discipline, and by 1705
the inexperienced hordes which had fought at Narva had been
transformed into an efficient, well-equipped force, the infantry
numbering 40,000 and the cavalry 20,000 men. In that year an
improved method of recruitment was introduced whereby annual
levies were held and every twenty households provided one soldier. These recruits were locally trained in groups of about 500
by officers no longer engaged in active service. The burdens imposed by such levies, the constant demands for labour in the shipyards and elsewhere, together with heavy taxation, caused
widespread discontent; rebellious outbreaks were to be a constant
problem during following years. Not least of Peter's difficulties
in his largely military and naval programme was the perpetual
lack of skilled labour, and in January 1701 he established a
School of Mathematics and Navigation in Moscow in the hope of
doing something to remedy this deficiency. Furthermore, in
April 1702, aiming to attract officers and skilled craftsmen, Peter
issued a proclamation which invited foreigners (except Jews) to
settle in Russia, offering them free passage, their own law-courts,
and freedom of worship. Amidst all this activity, the Czar found
time to deal with two practices particularly objectionable to
foreigners from the west. Henceforth deformed babies were not
to be killed at birth and marriage was no longer to be arranged
according to old Muscovite custom, the parties having no voice
in the matter.

With every year Peter grew stronger, and he took full advantage of Charles's prolonged absence in Poland to reconquer
Russia's ancient outlet to the Baltic, at the same time keeping

Augustus supplied with reinforcements. Thus at a meeting between the allies in February 1701, Peter ever-fearful of being forced to face the Swedes alone before he was fully prepared, or of being attacked simultaneously by Swedes and Poles (many of the latter regarded Russia with hatred), agreed to supply Augustus with between 15,000 and 20,000 troops as well as substantial subsidies which he could ill afford. Meanwhile in the north, the Russians, seizing the initiative in the face of small Swedish forces, who could scarcely hope to resist for long consistent attacks on such an extensive frontier, devastated Livonia and set about conquering Ingria. October 1702 saw the fall of Noteborg, a fortress on the river Neva guarding the entrance to lake Ladoga, which Russia had long coveted. After this success, Peter established the first Russian newspaper in an attempt to keep his subjects (hitherto left in total ignorance) informed of events. In May 1703 a small Swedish naval squadron was destroyed at the entrance to the Neva, and the whole of Ingria was soon in Russian hands. In the same month, Peter laid the foundations of a new city at the mouth of the Neva – St Petersburg – which he was later to make the Russian capital.

The decision to establish his 'paradise' on a swampy river delta, prone to floods, in a cold, foggy, climate, was undoubtedly a hasty one. Other, far more suitable, sites in the Baltic area could have been developed with less difficulty and expense, of the magnitude of which he had at first no conception. As the obstacles became evident, Peter, nothing daunted, pressed forward with even greater determination, sparing neither money nor lives to see his dream fulfilled. Many thousands of peasants were drafted to the almost uninhabited area where they laboured under appalling conditions, ravaged by disease and constantly harassed by Swedish attacks. Millions of tons of stone had to be hauled there, for Peter had decreed that his new city, designed in Dutch style, should be constructed of more permanent materials than wood, while innumerable piles were driven into the waterlogged, barren ground. As an entrance for foreigners and as a port, Peter had great hopes of St Petersburg and, by cutting customs dues to less than those levied at Archangel and to half the amount previously levied by the Swedes, he lost no time in persuading merchants from the west to call there: soon ships from England and Holland began to come regularly to the city. Simultaneously a Russian Baltic fleet was under construction and a naval base, Kronstadt, was established eight miles away to guard the approaches of the river Neva.

1704 was a sad year in the north for the Swedes. In May the Russians destroyed a Swedish naval force on lake Peipus and in July they took the fortress of Dorpat in Livonia. Since April, Narva itself had been under siege by a large Russian force under General Ogilvie, a competent and experienced officer recently recruited from imperial service, and eventually, after heroic resistance, this important stronghold capitulated. The Swedish defence system in the Baltic had thus crumbled away and only the coastal towns of Riga, Pernau and Reval remained. Yet Charles stayed in Poland whither he was apparently hoping to lure the main Russian forces and annihilate them, in his usual fashion, with one devastating blow; and this wish seemed about to be fulfilled. Peter had made a new agreement with Augustus in 1704, promising him 12,000 troops and fresh subsidies, and in 1705 the Russian army under General Ogilvie moved into Lithuania, taking up winter quarters in Grodno where it was joined by both Peter and Augustus.

After the recent Swedish failures in Livonia and Ingria, Charles was no doubt considerably encouraged by the news in the summer of 1705 that a Russian force had been heavily defeated by the Swedes under General Lewenhaupt in Courland. Now, having left a small force of 10,000 men to guard Poland and the Saxon frontier, commanded by the distinguished General Rehnsköld, Charles proclaimed a winter campaign and made all speed towards Grodno. This news disturbed the Czar, who had recently returned to Moscow, and who did not feel ready to risk his new army, and indeed his whole policy, in a pitched battle with the Swedes. Thus when Charles arrived before Grodno in January he discovered that Ogilvie had done much to make it impregnable and he was forced to retreat a little in order to ensure supplies for the Swedish army. Augustus was thereby enabled to march out with

5,000 men on his way to join the main Saxon force of 18,000 under
General Schulenburg, who had been ordered to attack Rehnsköld.
Both Peter and Augustus were confident that Rehnsköld would
be wiped out and that the victorious Saxon army would then
march to the aid of Ogilvie at Grodno. But at Fraustadt, on the
border between Silesia and Poland, Rehnsköld on 3 February
1706 brilliantly defeated Schulenburg's army in two hours, and
Augustus's plans came to nothing. Peter was now even more
worried about his army, and for two months sent constant mess-
ages to Ogilvie to retreat, if necessary abandoning the artillery.
The latter, knowing the risks, was obstinate, but at length, on
24 March, the Russians left Grodno, and they were only saved
by the breaking of the ice of the river Niemen which carried away
the bridge constructed by the Swedes, over which Charles had
intended to throw his army at the first signs of an enemy
retreat. By the time the bridge was rebuilt, Ogilvie had four days
start, and although Charles forced-marched his army over appalling terrain at amazing speed, he was forced to abandon the
chase at Pinsk. The Russian army fell back to Kiev, and Charles,
weary of pursuing retreating armies all over Poland, turned
westwards. In August 1706, having joined Rehnsköld, he marched into Saxony. He established his headquarters at a castle
named Altranstädt, a short distance from Leipzig, and here the
ambassadors of Augustus, who was now faced with the prospect
of losing his electorate as well as his kingdom, signed a humiliating
treaty with Charles in September. Augustus renounced the Polish
throne, recognized Stanislas, gave up his alliance with Peter,
surrendered Patkul, who was later cruelly tortured and broken
on the wheel, and agreed to maintain the Swedish army in
Saxony. His punishment was complete.

The arrival of the Swedish king in the centre of Europe, fresh
from his victories and triumphs, caused a tremendous stir. He
was by repute a military genius; already, at the age of twenty-
five, he was a legend, and he came at the head of his equally
famous veteran troops, undefeated, and apparently, invincible.
A critical point had been reached in the War of the Spanish
Succession, and the possible intervention, on one side or the

other, of the formidable, highly disciplined Caroline army, under
the command of its gifted king, was a matter of the utmost concern to western generals and diplomats. Thus Altranstädt, until
the summer of 1707, was to be the focal point of Europe. French
hopes grew as there seemed increasing prospect of a serious
quarrel between Charles and the Emperor. The allies, indeed,
were sufficiently worried to sanction the journey to Altranstädt
of their most impressive envoy, the great Duke of Marlborough
himself, victor of Blenheim and Ramillies, and a first-class diplomatist. In February 1707 he had written to Heinsius, the Grand
Pensionary of Holland:

If you thought it might be of any advantage to the Public, I should
not scruple the trouble of a journey as far as Saxony, to wait on the
King, and endeavour, if need be, to set him right, or at least to pene-
trate his design, that we might take the justest measures we can not
to be surprised.[3]

Little is known of the meeting which took place between Charles
XII and the Duke of Marlborough in April, but the latter divined
correctly that Charles was mainly concerned with Russia, and
that the possibility of his intervening in the western war was
remote. Nevertheless, for a while, the situation was tense, for
Charles had several causes of complaint against the Emperor, the
most important of which was the persecution of Protestants in
imperial Silesia, thus violating the Peace of Westphalia of which
Sweden was a guarantor. The Emperor, under the circumstances
in no position to bargain, finally agreed to all Charles's demands
and, in August 1707, an agreement was signed which guaranteed
the rights of the Silesian Protestants and restored to them one
hundred and thirty-four churches. In the same month, Charles,
at the head of the largest and most magnificent army he had ever
commanded, a total of nearly 45,000 men, marched eastward
out of Saxony towards Russia.

Peter feared the Swedish king, and throughout 1706 he made
anxious overtures for peace. In January he offered to surrender

3. Quoted by Winston S. Churchill, *The Life of John Churchill, Duke of
Marlborough*, Vol. III, Harrap (London, 1936; reprinted, 2 vols., 1966).

all his Baltic conquests except St Petersburg and the river Neva, and to provide the allies in the west with 30,000 of his best troops, if only they would negotiate on his behalf with Charles. At the end of the year the Czar sent Matvieev to London, where he arrived in May 1707, to repeat the offer and investigate the possibility of bribing the chief ministers. To Prince Eugene, the imperial commander, as well as to Rakóczy, the leader of the Hungarian rebellion against the Emperor, he offered the Polish throne! He approached France, Denmark and Prussia, seeking mediation in every possible quarter, but he sought in vain. In the first place, Charles would have nothing of mediation; he demanded unconditional surrender which Peter consistently refused to consider. Secondly, despite their successes in the Baltic provinces, Russian troops were still regarded almost as figures of fun in Europe, doubtless unable to resist a Swedish onslaught, and thus of little value to the western powers. Finally, if neither France nor the allies could persuade Charles to join them, they would much prefer him to depart eastwards to settle accounts with Russia, rather than feel free to act in the west. Peter, therefore, had every reason to feel harassed. He could find no help in Europe; he had called down upon his head the terrible vengeance of an implacable foe; and he was threatened, at the very moment when Charles was moving against him, with a serious rebellion in the Cossack lands. Surely he was doomed. Charles, for his part, was certain of victory. Ignoring suggestions that he might recover the Baltic provinces, it had become evident, by the spring of 1708, that he had decided to march to Moscow, to the very heart of the Russian empire, where he would dictate peace to the Czar. The Finnish professor, Eino Jutikkala makes this comment:

He set forth on the road that Gustavus Adolphus had avoided – the same road that Napoleon and Hitler later followed.[4]

4. Eino Jutikkala, *A History of Finland*, Thames and Hudson (London, 1962).

Further Reading

Frans Bengtsson, *The Life of Charles XII, King of Sweden 1697–1718*. Macmillan (London, 1960).

R. Nisbet Bain, *Charles XII*. Putnam (New York and London, 1895).

Ian Grey, *Peter the Great, Emperor of All Russia*. Hodder (London, 1962).

Vasili Klyuchevsky, *Peter the Great*. Macmillan (London, 1958).

B. H. Sumner, *Peter the Great and the Emergence of Russia*. English Universities Press (London, 1951).

B. H. Sumner, 'Peter the Great'. *History* (March 1947).

Ian Grey, 'Peter the Great and the Creation of the Russian Navy'. *History Today* (September 1961).

See also pages 44–5.

PART VII
The Great Northern War (2)—
The Collapse of the Swedish
Baltic Empire

[33] THE PROGRESS OF THE WAR TO
THE BATTLE OF POLTAVA (1709)

With the advantage of hindsight it is a temptation to regard
Charles XII's expedition to Russia as a reckless adventure. But
this was not the case at the time. The situation facing Peter the
Great was indeed extremely grave, a fact of which he was only
too aware. Wide resentment had been kindled among the unedu-
cated, superstitious people of Russia by his westernizing policies;
discontent seethed as the weight of taxation increased and the
burdens of labour and military service grew intolerable. In particular the institution of revenue officers whose duty it was to
prevent tax evasion, provoked general hostility. The Czar himself
was most unpopular and rumour circulated that he was the Anti-
christ, or a changeling, probably the son of Lefort. Open rebellion
had broken out in the Astrakhan region, and in 1707 the Cossacks
of the Don river revolted. For a year the government struggled to
regain control of the area, while at the same time rebellion spread
to the Urals, threatening Peter's new iron works. Fortunately the
worst was over before issue was joined with Charles, but the
Dnieper Cossacks were also known to be unreliable and the
Tatars of the Crimea as well as the Turks were always ready to

strike another blow at Muscovy. Indeed a Swedish victory at this stage could well have resulted in the downfall of Peter and the destruction of all his work.

Charles XII's designs were on a grand scale. His main army of about 35,000 men was to aim at the heart of Russia while eight regiments were left behind in Poland under General Krassow to cooperate with Stanislas Leszczynski and any troops he might raise. After suppressing disturbances there, they were to march to the Ukraine where a rising of the Cossacks was being engineered and contact made with the Tatars and Turks. Meanwhile General Lewenhaupt, in command of the Swedish army based at Riga, was to move south with a large supply train and join up with the main army. Simultaneously another force, under General Lybecker, should invade Ingria from Finland and with the help of the Swedish fleet capture St Petersburg.

But the very magnitude of these plans made them impracticable; they included too many incalculable factors; inevitably much depended upon chance. Charles, who took little account of human limitations, seemed unaware of the extent to which even the best army is undermined by constant forced marches over difficult and unknown terrain and by lengthy periods away from home. Moreover even the King of Sweden could not control the weather and the troops were to suffer untold hardships. He underestimated also the enormous difficulties involved in maintaining communications over such a far-flung theatre of operations. Always supremely confident, he did not forsee the consequences which might follow if even one part of his vast project went astray, but to his bitter disappointment he was destined to witness the failure of all his schemes. A succession of miscalculations and blunders, together with sheer bad luck, resulted not in the ruin of Peter but in the destruction of the fine Swedish army and ultimately of the Swedish Baltic empire.

During the summer of 1708 Charles made his way through Poland towards the river Dnieper, aiming at the northern road to Moscow by way of Smolensk. The Russians gradually retired before him not attempting to give battle but laying waste the land with the utmost thoroughness. Meanwhile the Swedes suffered under frightful conditions amid the marshes and mud-bound forests of the region. On 30 June the two armies fought a fierce engagement at Holovzin, west of the Dnieper and, thanks to Charles's tactical skill and a brilliant cavalry action led by Rehnsköld, the Swedes, in what was to be Charles XII's last successful pitched battle, defeated the large Russian force, although conditions prevented its complete destruction. The way was now open to the Dnieper and in July Charles set up camp at Mohilev on that river to recover from recent hardships and to await Lewenhaupt upon whose supply train and reinforcements further large-scale action depended.

But Lewenhaupt was making extraordinarily slow progress and the King waited in vain. In August Charles crossed the Dnieper and attempted, by moving to the south-east and then turning northwards, to outflank the Russian forces which were covering Smolensk. But the Czar had carried out his scorched-earth policy as thoroughly in his own territory as he had previously done in Poland, and by September, when Charles arrived at Tatarsk on the Russian border, it was clear that he could proceed no further towards Smolensk, nor indeed remain where he was. At a council of war he could not be persuaded to retreat to the Dnieper to look for Lewenhaupt, accepting erroneous reports that the latter was near at hand. Therefore, expecting the general to catch up, Charles turned south towards the unravaged region of Severia.

In so doing Charles made a serious blunder. Lewenhaupt was still far behind and was left in great danger by the King's action. At the end of September the general was overtaken by the Russians and at the battle of Lesnaya the entire baggage train and half the Swedish force of 11,000 were lost. Vasili Klyuchevsky[1] comments that the outcome of Poltava was made possible by the battle of Lesnaya and there is no doubt that Charles, had he been successfully reinforced by Lewenhaupt, would have been formidable. As it was the morale of the Russian troops rose, while the Swedes, practically starving and weakened by terrible marches through apparently endless forests, arrived in Severia

1. Vasili Klyuchevsky, *Peter the Great*, Macmillan (London, 1958).

only to find that their advance detachment had failed to prevent
the Russians from arriving first and laying waste the entire area.
The remnants of Lewenhaupt's army at last joined Charles but
Severia was now no place for winter quarters: the Swedes were
forced to move south once more, into the Ukraine.

While Lewenhaupt met with disaster, General Lybecker completely failed in Ingria. But despite these disappointments,
Charles, having postponed his attack on Moscow until the following year, looked forward confidently to securing supplies in the
Ukraine, as well as gaining valuable support from the Cossacks.
Negotiations had in fact been proceeding for some time with
Mazeppa, the powerful chief of the Dnieper Cossacks, who had
many thousands of skilled horsemen at his disposal and who was
treated with considerable respect by his overlord, the Czar. He
had been loyal to Moscow for many years, but the increasing
burdens imposed by Peter, together, perhaps, with a desire to
be on the winning side, led him to seize the opportunity provided
by the approach of the Swedes to make a bid for independence.
Had he successfully joined Charles and raised the Ukraine, the
result of the Poltava campaign might have been very different.
But when Mazeppa eventually arrived in the Swedish camp in
mid-October, he came as a fugitive, with only a small number of
loyal supporters. Wrongly imagining that Peter knew of his
treachery, he had fled in panic on hearing that the Russian armies
were moving south, led by Menshikov, the Czar's right-hand man,
whom Mazeppa particularly feared and hated. The Russians,
who reached the Cossack capital Baturin before the Swedes,
sacked the town early in November and deprived Charles of the
much needed provisions and gunpowder stored there. Thus the
Ukraine was subdued and the King was surrounded by enemies
where he had expected to find friends and allies. It was a bitter
blow.

Charles's optimism, however, did not desert him. The Ukraine
provided adequate supplies and quarters were established at
Romne where Charles awaited the arrival of reinforcements from
Poland under Krassow and Stanislas Leszczynski. Efforts were
made to draw the Tatars and Turks into the enterprise and, al-

though the Russian army was demonstrably improved as a fighting force, the Czar faced considerable danger. But now Charles was overtaken by his worst misfortune – the weather. The winter of 1708–9 was throughout Europe the most severe in living memory, and in the Ukraine it was incomparably fierce. The sufferings of the Swedish army were indescribable: hundreds froze to death and thousands were injured by frost-bite and disease. As a result, when Charles took up quarters in the new year between the rivers Psiol and Vorskla, two tributaries of the Dnieper, his force was seriously depleted with a fighting strength of only about 24,000 men. An attempt to cross the Vorskla and move towards Moscow was thwarted by floods which came with a temporary thaw in February and, while the Swedes waited for better weather, hope, never more than a bare possibility, that help would soon arrive from Stanislas and the Poles, receded still further. A Russian force was dispatched to cut off any advance by General Krassow, and Peter staged impressive manoeuvres at Azof to discourage the Sultan from coming to Charles's aid. In the end the only allies the Swedish king could enlist were the Zaporogian Cossacks, unruly horsemen who lived further to the south; but shortly they too were crushed by the Russians.

Charles's position was thus precarious in the extreme; all communication with the rest of Europe had been lost and there was no prospect of aid. Yet his courage never failed him. Refusing to consider retreat, he prepared for the summer campaign when he would deliver the final blow. Indeed, with supplies once more running low and with numbers constantly dwindling, an encounter with the Russian army would inevitably be decisive for the Swedes one way or the other: victory would mean the consummation of Charles's plans; defeat, the loss of all. When, on 1 May 1709, Charles laid siege to the fortress of Poltava, situated on the middle Vorskla, he hoped that Peter would at last be tempted to fight a pitched battle.

Sure enough, towards the end of May, Peter began concentrating his army of about 45,000 well-seasoned troops to the north of Poltava. Charles had only about 22,000, although remembering previous engagements with the Russians he refused to be daunted. But he was soon to discover that his opponents, as a result of the Czar's military reforms, bore no resemblance to the untrained masses he had encountered at Narva. Moreover, apart from vastly superior numbers, the Russians had far more artillery and ammunition, and in contrast to the Swedes, their morale was high. Even before the momentous battle itself, calamity befell the Swedish army. The King was seriously wounded in the foot during a preliminary skirmish and henceforth was unable to direct operations. Frans Bengtsson argues that from this injury 'stemmed the defeat at Poltava'. Certainly Field-Marshal Rehnsköld, who took over the command, able though he was, could not take the place of the King. Moreover he was quite unable to see eye to eye with Lewenhaupt. Thus the Swedes lacked the calm, skilful leadership to which they had become so accustomed. In addition, definite news now came that no help could be expected from Poland. A bold plan of attack was none the less worked out and, on 28 June 1709, 17,000 Swedes began the advance. The rest of his army Charles had left behind either at the fortress of Poltava, or guarding the baggage and communications in the rear.

From the first, things went seriously wrong. Charles, transported in a litter, could give no effective help, while Rehnsköld omitted to brief the leaders properly, and Lewenhaupt, in particular, failed to cooperate with him. An attempt to surprise the Russians under cover of darkness was unsuccessful and catastrophe shortly followed. One third of the infantry was stranded among the cleverly constructed redoubts that Peter had positioned in the path of the Swedes, and was soon annihilated. The rest of the Swedish infantry, with little assistance from the cavalry, was overwhelmed, after a fierce struggle, despite courageous endeavours by Lewenhaupt. Swedish losses were very heavy; about 7,000 officers and men were killed and some 2,700 captured, including Rehnsköld. The King himself narrowly escaped seizure, and about 8,000 survivors eventually left the field. After joining those who had remained behind, a total of 15,000 men, including sick and wounded began the retreat. On arrival at the Dnieper, the King, thoroughly exhausted, was persuaded to leave the army and cross the river with a few hundred followers. He would then make all haste to Turkey in the hope of gaining support. Meanwhile the rest, too numerous to cross the Dnieper with the few available boats, would cross instead the Vorskla, under Lewenhaupt's command, and proceed southeastwards to the Crimea, later joining the King. But morale was at its lowest and Lewenhaupt had a hard task maintaining discipline. In the end he appears to have lost his head when the Russian cavalry caught up, and believing the enemy to be three times larger than it actually was, surrendered, making no attempt to resist. The famous Caroline army was no more; and the Swedish veterans were to face new hardships in captivity. Peter I wrote of his great victory:

Now with the help of God the final stone in the foundation of St Petersburg has been laid.[2]

2. Quoted by Ian Grey, *Peter the Great, Emperor of all Russia*, Hodder (London, 1962), p. 305.

[34] THE RENEWAL OF THE COALITION AGAINST SWEDEN

The immediate effect of Poltava was to give Sweden's enemies a second chance. Within three months, the Czar, Augustus and Frederick IV renewed their alliances to keep Sweden, in the words of the agreement between Saxony and Denmark, 'within her proper limits'. Prussia was approached once more, but Frederick I, though promising his friendship, still refused to take up arms against Charles XII. An even more significant result of the battle was that the rest of Europe was forced, for the first time, to take account of Russia in international affairs. Henceforth the Czar's influence was supreme in Poland where Augustus was restored,

Stanislas and General Krassow taking refuge in Swedish Pomerania. Moreover in 1710 Peter began operations in earnest on the Baltic seaboard. Carelia was overrun and the strategically vital fortress of Viborg fell in June. In July, after a lengthy siege, Riga capitulated, and during the rest of this year Pernau and Reval and Kexholm on lake Ladoga were taken, completing the Russian conquest of Sweden's Baltic possessions. In October Peter married his niece Anna to the Duke of Courland, and when the latter died two months later, a Russian garrison was installed. The year 1710 also saw considerable growth of the Russian navy, and from this time onwards the fear that Sweden would be destroyed and that Peter would soon dominate the Baltic increased rapidly in western Europe, and particularly in Great Britain, so dependent upon that region for naval supplies. Sweden was unable to take action against Russia in the east because Denmark once more seized the apparently opportune moment to launch an attack upon the Scanian provinces. A force of some 15,000 men crossed the Sound in November 1709, but in the following March this rather disorganized expedition was unexpectedly routed at Hälsingborg by the Swedes under Magnus Stenbock, the Governor General of Skåne.

[35] CHARLES RESISTS TO THE LAST

The success at Hälsingborg proved that Sweden's position was far from hopeless, and that it would take more than a single disaster to destroy the strong military state. Moreover the maritime powers had no wish to see Sweden's power in the north destroyed completely and there still seemed some prospect of aid against Russia from the Turks. On the other hand the destruction of the army at Poltava and the flight of the King were grievous blows and seriously undermined Sweden's prestige in Europe. But Charles appears to have been blind to the magnitude of the problems now facing his country, and his determination to resist to the end, his inability to compromise, his obstinate adherence to impractical schemes, and his very absence from the realm at a time of desperate need did Sweden even greater harm during the remaining nine years of his reign.

At first, however, not only did Charles expect early success, but also the rest of Europe feared a Swedish recovery. The King himself still inspired dread and the Swedish troops in Pomerania excited considerable apprehension, a feeling which increased with the victory at Hälsingborg and thus the prospect of reinforcements from Sweden. In fact the possibility that Germany might once more become the scene of hostilities between Sweden and her numerous foes, inevitably resulting in the withdrawal of valuable troops from the coalition fighting against France, led the maritime powers and the Emperor to sign the famous 'Neutrality Compact' at The Hague in March 1710. It was agreed that Sweden's German possessions should neither be invaded, nor used as bases for a Swedish offensive, and that, if necessary, force should be used to carry out this arrangement. This proposal was generally accepted and the Swedish Council, bearing in mind the exhausted state of the country, was also in agreement. But Charles violently repudiated the scheme and subsequently removed all control over diplomatic and foreign affairs from the hands of his councillors in Stockholm. In a formal protest he stated that relying on God's help and the justice of his cause, he would employ all the resources within his power to defeat his enemies. Towards England Charles was particularly hostile. A defensive treaty had been concluded with William III in 1700 by which it was agreed that 6,000 troops should be sent to aid the King of Sweden if he were attacked. Charles now made repeated, though fruitless, demands that these terms should be fulfilled. Indeed, far from adopting a defensive attitude, he acted against Russia's conquest of the Baltic Provinces by prohibiting all trade with the area and commissioning privateers to prey on any merchantmen who might be tempted to defy the ban. Then, at the end of the year, came the news that Turkey had once more been prevailed upon to declare war on Russia.

Russia and Turkey at war

Charles remained in Turkey for five years, first at Bender and
later at Adrianople. Received with honour and no little curiosity
by the Turks, he rapidly became the centre of a vigorous campaign against Russia in which he was supported by the Khan of
the Crimea, a vassal of the Sultan. The King still entertained
extravagant designs; his ultimate aim was to secure the support
of 50,000 Turks to march into Poland and unite with a new
Swedish army operating from Pomerania which was to be equipped and dispatched from Sweden at the earliest opportunity.
(Thus the intention of the Swedish Council to neutralize that
province was in complete opposition to Charles's plan.) A great
offensive against Russia was then to be put into operation. At
length the efforts of Charles and the Khan bore fruit, and the
Sultan, thoroughly alarmed at the sudden growth in Russian
power, agreed to war.

It was now Peter's turn to blunder: for a brief moment he was
almost at Charles's mercy, and had it not been for the timidity
of the Turkish Grand Vizier, the future of both monarchs might
still have been very different. The Czar, forced against his will
into the war with Turkey, made bold preparations. He called
upon the Balkan Christians to rise against their Moslem masters,
and marched towards the Danube into Moldavia. But the Balkan
Christians did not rise in force, nor did Peter gain over the rich
province of Wallachia. Moreover he was ignorant of the size and
location of the Turkish army (strongly supported by the Tatars
of the Crimea) and he failed to provide adequate provisions for
his troops. As a result, in July 1711, the Czar found himself surrounded and outnumbered by nearly five to one on the banks of
the river Pruth, a tributary of the Danube, and with only
enough supplies for a few days. This extraordinary situation was
apparently quite beyond the comprehension of the Grand
Vizier, terrified as he was by the proximity of the enemy, and he
received proposals of peace from the Russians with alacrity,
although the latter, fully aware that they could be rapidly star-
ved into surrender, entertained no hope that their offer would

be considered. Charles, hearing the news at his camp fifty miles away, dashed to the scene. But it was too late; peace had been signed and although the terms were humiliating they were far less severe than the Russians expected. Sweden gained nothing, although the Czar, in his instructions to his negotiators, had been prepared to surrender all his Baltic conquests, except Ingria, and also to recognize Stanislas Leszczynski as King of Poland if this should be necessary to satisfy the Turks. But the Sultan was content with much less, and by the provisions of the Peace of the Pruth, Peter returned the port of Azof, thus abandoning the fleet he had constructed at such a cost, promised not to interfere in Polish affairs and undertook to give Charles a free passage to Sweden. Highly disagreeable as this was to the Czar, it was an even greater disappointment to Charles; the chance of capturing Peter himself together with his whole army had been lost by a hair's breadth.

Still the King did not give up and aided by the fact that Peter continued to interfere in Poland, war was twice more declared on Russia by the Turks. But, by 1713, Charles had outstayed his welcome and in February of that year occurred the famous 'affray', an amazing incident in which Charles defended his house for 8 hours with only 40 followers against a Turkish army of 12,000 with artillery. The Turks were now tired of war and, with the surrender of the latest Swedish army in northern Europe, and the end of the War of the Spanish Succession (Austria now being free to turn her attention to Turkey), the Sultan signed a definitive peace with Russia in July 1713 at Adrianople.

Sweden's desperate plight

While Sweden's absolute monarch remained many miles away (he lingered in Turkey for another fifteen months after the peace was signed), the situation at home grew desperate and a strong hand was urgently needed. Taxes were intolerable; recent harvests had failed and the plague had taken its toll. Expenditure was nearly three times the income of the government, and yet Charles continued to demand a newly equipped army to march into Poland in support of his schemes against Russia. At last in July 1712, with the utmost sacrifice, a force of 9,000 men was collected under the command of Stenbock and it crossed the Baltic to Rügen in the autumn. But the Danish fleet succeeded in destroying the Swedish transports and thus Stenbock was deprived of supplies essential for any campaign in Poland. Furthermore, Pomerania itself was hard pressed as in the summer of the previous year Russians, Danes and Saxons had attacked Sweden's German possessions. In 1712 a strong offensive was launched by the Russians and Saxons against Stralsund, Wismar and Stettin. Meanwhile the Danes attacked Bremen, and the Elector of Hanover occupied Verden, unwilling to see the King of Denmark established in both these strategically important provinces which controlled the mouths of the rivers Weser and Elbe and divided Hanover from the sea. Clearly an advance into Poland by Stenbock was out of the question despite reinforcements in Pomerania. Indeed the new Swedish army was dangerously isolated, threatened by the Danes approaching from the west and the Russians and Saxons from the east. Stenbock decided to attack the Danes, who were the weaker and, after a fierce fight, he completely routed them at Gadebusch in Mecklenburg. But this did little to improve the situation and Stenbock was forced to retreat to Jutland, pursued by his three enemies. In February 1713 he took refuge in the Holstein-Gottorp fortress of Tönning, thus giving Frederick IV the opportunity to occupy all the Duke's lands. But Stenbock's position was hopeless and in May 1713 he surrendered with his army to the King of Denmark, by whom he was kept in solitary confinement until his death some years later.

Such was the end of the last Swedish army to be sent to Germany, its gallant leader sacrificed. It was now clear to everyone except Charles that the nation could not survive much longer against such powerful opposition. But the King, unyielding, rejected all offers of mediation from the maritime powers, as well as a proposal of alliance on very reasonable terms from Prussia. He absolutely refused to make the smallest concession. On the contrary, he instructed that the economic blockade of the

Baltic provinces should be rigorously enforced and this angered
Britain and Holland, both of whom were originally disposed in
his favour. Moreover, Prussia, ruled since February by King
Frederick William I, took an important step towards Charles's
enemies when it was agreed that she should occupy Stettin
(which had fallen to the Russians in September 1713) for the
duration of the war. It was during this year also that Peter
undertook the conquest of Finland, an extremely valuable part
of Sweden's empire, not only as a source of manpower and raw
materials but also as a bulwark for Sweden proper. Helsingfors
and Äbo (then the capital) fell and in the spring of 1714 the
Swedes were utterly overwhelmed at the battle of Storkyro.
In July, off Cape Hango, Peter won his first important naval
victory when he wholly outmanoeuvred the Swedish fleet: as a
result the Russians were able to land on the Åland islands situated very near the Swedish mainland. Of this victory Peter was
particularly proud. He compared it to Poltava and rejoiced that
he had now crushed both Sweden's army and navy. By the end
of 1714 Finland was completely in Russian hands but, despite
these successes, Peter failed to deliver a really decisive blow
against Sweden in the Baltic, a blow which would have shortened
the war, and brought even greater reward. He became too involved in German politics and pursued an essentially cautious
policy, always seeking allies, even when they were as feeble and
untrustworthy as Denmark and Saxony.

1714 was indeed a black year for Sweden. All that remained of
her empire were Wismar, Stralsund and Rügen, while Denmark
and Russia were planning a combined attack on the Scanian
provinces. Moreover the Elector of Hanover was now openly
scheming with Denmark, Russia and Prussia to divide up Sweden's
former possessions and, in June, Prussia and Russia mutually
guaranteed the territories which they had already gained from
Sweden. Two months later the Elector of Hanover succeeded to
the throne of England inevitably giving that country's policy a
new slant. But, even before this, a British squadron had been
ordered to the Baltic to escort merchantmen fearful of Swedish
privateers. In fact Charles's commercial policy was forcing the

British government to take up an increasingly anti-Swedish position, despite the official view which was anxious about the sudden development of Russia and is summed up in the words of Henry St John (later Viscount Bolingbroke):

We must do what we can to save him (Charles XII) from that ruin which he seems so earnestly to seek, and not suffer the balance of the north to be destroyed.[3]

In November 1714, George, as Elector of Hanover, signed an agreement with Frederick William I of Prussia by which they agreed to maintain each other in the territories they had acquired. Consequently Charles now faced two more enemies eager to share in the spoils; at the same time the maritime powers grew hostile.

It was in this month (November 1714) that Charles XII at last unexpectedly reappeared at Stralsund. He had completed the journey from Turkey dressed as a courier with two companions at extraordinary speed, covering nearly 100 miles a day. His realm was on the verge of dissolution. It seemed to the Swedes, with invasion in sight, that their king was completely indifferent to their plight, and at an unconstitutional meeting of the Estates in the winter of 1713–14, it was proposed that peace negotiations should be set on foot (the King having expressly forbidden such a course) and that Charles's younger sister, Ulrica, should be placed at the head of the government. The situation was saved ultimately by the firmness of the Chancellor, Count Arvid Horn, and all was forgotten, at least for the present, amid the tremendous enthusiasm which greeted Charles's arrival once more upon Swedish soil.

Confident as ever, the King, in February 1715, issued a 'Privateer Ordinance' which stepped up the activities of the Swedish pirates in the Baltic. As a result the maritime powers ordered their fleets to that sea in the summer and, although Admiral Norris, in command of the British squadron, had no instructions to act against Sweden, he was well aware that George I, as Elector of Hanover, wished to prevent the relief of Stralsund by

3. Quoted by J. F. Chance, *George I and the Northern War*, Smith, Elder (London, 1909).

the Swedes. Accordingly, he left a detachment with the Danes and thus gave the latter superiority of numbers in the western Baltic. The rest of the fleet sailed to Reval where it met the Russian navy and three weeks of festivities ensued; but the Czar was to be disappointed in his hopes of working actively with George I. Meanwhile, in January, negotiations had been resumed between Hanover, Denmark and Prussia for a league against Sweden. At last, after much wrangling, a confederation was formed in the summer by the three states who partitioned Sweden's German possessions between them. Hanover was to buy Bremen and Verden from Denmark while the latter would receive Rügen and the northern part of Swedish Pomerania as well as full control of Schleswig. Prussia would gain Stettin and the rest of Pomerania while Wismar (in Mecklenburg) was to be a free city of the Empire. Prussia had declared war on Sweden in April and Hanover followed suit in October; both made agreements with Russia that same autumn. Charles was now at open war with most of northern Europe and Stralsund was doomed. The Danes prevented the Swedes from sending aid by sea and after the fall of Rügen capitulation of the fortress was only a matter of time. Finally in December 1715, after a heroic resistance, the King remaining in the front line day and night, Stralsund fell to the enemy. Charles escaped two days earlier and, narrowly avoiding capture by the Danish fleet, he landed in Sweden after an absence of fifteen years.

By now Charles was acquiring a reputation for madness. All Sweden's trans-Baltic possessions (except Wismar which was soon to fall) – Pomerania, Bremen and Verden, the Baltic provinces and Finland – had been lost, and yet peace was far from his thoughts. As soon as he arrived in his hard-pressed land he set about gathering troops and supplies for another campaign: this time he hoped that the conquest of Norway would either provide compensation for his losses or put him in a stronger bargaining position. Consequently, in March 1716 he occupied Christiana (Oslo) but he met with stiff opposition at the fortress of Fredrikshald situated on the frontier further south. After the young and daring Norwegian naval captain, Tordenskjöld, had destroyed the Swedish transports in harbour a few miles away, Charles withdrew from Norway, at least for the time. His presence was in any case required in Skåne which was threatened with imminent invasion.

Division among Sweden's enemies

There seemed, indeed, no prospect of an end to the war unless Charles could be decisively defeated in Sweden herself, but the differences among her various enemies were so difficult to compose that a common plan of action seemed remote. Ultimately, however, in June 1716, Frederick IV and Peter I signed a definite agreement to invade Skåne, while the British fleet, once again in the Baltic, having received no satisfaction from Charles on the matter of privateers, was instructed by George to cooperate with the navies of Denmark and Russia. In July Peter arrived in Copenhagen and 30,000 Russian and 23,000 Danish troops gathered in Zealand. But long delays occurred, and towards the end of September Peter suddenly announced that it was too late in the season and that the enterprise should be postponed until the following year. He had recently reconnoitred the Swedish coast and discovered that the enemy was strongly entrenched. Moreover he still feared Charles, and was unsure of the reliability of his allies, Denmark and Hanover. He was probably right in deciding that the risk was too great, for Charles had taken every precaution against invasion including removing all supplies from Skåne and arranging for the complete evacuation of towns in the area. But Peter's decision caused a great outcry from the Danes while George I was particularly incensed by Peter's intention to quarter his troops in Mecklenburg. In the previous April the Czar had married his niece Catherine to the Duke of Mecklenburg and had promised the Duke military aid against his rebellious nobles. This interference in German affairs was a serious blunder on Peter's part: it was the main obstacle to cooperation between himself and George I and it led to a wave of anti-Russian feeling in Britain, a feeling strengthened by rumours that Peter might support the Jacobites. This fear was exaggerated but the Czar did play with the idea more than once. Thus the league against Sweden was breaking up. Peter was besides on bad terms with the Danes not only over the invasion scheme but also because they had refused to allow Russian troops into Wismar when it fell in the previous spring. Nor was there any love lost between the Danes and the Hanoverians. Henceforth conflict in the north was as much diplomatic as military, and as much between the members of the confederation as against Sweden herself, a state of affairs which Charles XII's new minister, Baron von Görtz, sought to turn to advantage.

The 'Grand Vizier', as Görtz was called in Sweden, was officially in the service of the Duke of Holstein-Gottorp, but when Charles returned to Stralsund he offered to employ himself in the King's interests. Extremely able and resourceful, he had a great admiration for Charles and was indefatigable in his service, never daunted by the apparent hopelessness of Sweden's position. It was this quality which no doubt appealed to the King. Moreover, in great contrast to his master, Görtz was a brilliant diplomatist and he was soon in control of Sweden's foreign policy. He took over, in addition, all matters of home administration, superseding the Council and the old government organization and ignoring all opposition to get his many schemes into operation. A new department, the 'Purchasing Commission', was created to regulate economic matters – commerce, the metal industries, agriculture, all came under its jurisdiction. A token copper coinage was introduced to replace the silver coins withdrawn by the government, but over-issue led to unstable prices. Every possible means was employed to raise money; forced loans increased; taxation grew heavier and at the same time conscription for military service was harshly enforced. Görtz was soon regarded as the source of all evil and he became the object of widespread hatred. Certainly Charles gave him a very free hand and for a while his methods produced results. But it was impossible to find sufficient money at home to increase the Swedish fleet and Görtz undertook to raise it abroad. But the only purse which he found open was that of the discontented English Jacobites, and both he and the Swedish Minister in London, Gyllenborg, became involved in

intrigues against the Hanoverian régime. However, the British
government was well aware of these machinations and early in
1717 Gyllenborg was imprisoned and the arrest of Görtz procured
in the Netherlands.

George I used this incident to rouse enthusiasm in the British
Parliament for his policy in northern Europe, and for the equip-
ping of a larger squadron to go to the Baltic in 1717, instructed
if necessary to attack the Swedish fleet. Britain was therefore
almost at war with Sweden. Yet hostility and jealousy of Peter's
growing power in the Baltic were increasing at the same time
and Stanhope, who took over British foreign policy during this
year, began to work to save something for Sweden from the
wreck. The Czar had, indeed, hoped that the discovery of the
Jacobite plot might incline George to work with him more closely,
but overtures came to nothing, and both George and Peter
opened separate negotiations with the Swedes.

Görtz, who had been released after six months, set himself to
use every means to widen the breach between George and Peter
and play one off against the other. But attempts on his part to
come to terms with Hanover failed because Charles absolutely
refused to consider ceding Bremen and Verden. Equally fruitless
were the prolonged discussions between Sweden and Russia
which began on one of the Åland islands in May 1718. Görtz
laboured on although he knew that the King would reject Russian
terms. In July he actually drew up a plan whereby Russia would
help Sweden seek compensation in Norway and Mecklenburg for
her losses in the eastern Baltic, and Peter was led to believe that
Charles had approved these proposals. When the Czar discovered
that Görtz had been concealing Charles's rejection of them for
some time, he made renewed overtures to Hanover. George wel-
comed these approaches for he feared that Alberoni, Spain's
chief minister, would draw both Charles and Peter into his schemes
against the Emperor (Britain's ally) and that they might make
common cause with the Jacobites.

Charles XII's last campaign (1718)

Charles XII had shown little interest in Görtz's negotiations for peace; his determination to fight on was insane. In the autumn of 1718 he once more led an army against south-western Norway while another force advanced simultaneously against Trondhjem. In November he laid siege to the fortress of Fredriksten near Fredrikshald and, on 30 November, while inspecting the trenches, he was killed instantaneously by a bullet which passed through his head. The Swedish army immediately evacuated Norway, the Trondhjem detachment suffering heavy losses from the extreme cold during the retreat. Exactly how Charles was killed is still a matter for controversy but the force of the bullet does suggest that it came from Swedish lines. Many accept the theory of murder, instigated, perhaps, by Charles's brother-in-law, Duke Frederick of Hesse, who immediately took steps to secure the crown for his wife, Ulrica Eleonora, Charles's younger sister. At all events, contemporaries must have seen Charles XII's death as an extreme anticlimax, a view held by Samuel Johnson who wrote in 1749:

> His fall was destined to a barren Strand,
> A petty Fortress and a dubious Hand;
> He left the Name at which the world grew pale,
> To point a Moral and adorn a Tale.[4]

Uncertainty about the succession to the Swedish throne, together with widespread disillusionment with autocratic government, gave the opponents of absolutism in Sweden the opportunity to transform the constitution, thereby limiting the power of the Crown, and inaugurating the so-called 'Age of Liberty'. Görtz was arrested immediately and executed for his crimes; he was alleged to have ignored the Council and divided the Swedish people from their king. His connexion with Holstein played a large part in frustrating the claim to the throne of the Duke of Holstein-Gottorp, the son of Charles XII's eldest sister who was now dead. Instead, Charles's younger sister, Ulrica Eleonora, whose husband had cooperated with the party opposing auto-

4. Samuel Johnson, *The Vanity of Human Wishes*.

cracy, was crowned Queen in May 1719, but only after she had
agreed to a new constitution, drawn up by the Riksdag (Estates).
In the following year, Ulrica Eleonora, who had revealed absolutist tendencies, was persuaded to abdicate in favour of her husband, who became King as Frederick I. Evidently it was hoped
that with no hereditary claim to the throne, he would prove more
docile. On his accession, the Crown's prerogatives were further
curtailed and henceforth the Riksdag was the supreme authority
in the state. The King was little more than the President of the
Council. He could be outvoted and he was compelled to select
Council members from a list drawn up by the Riksdag. The
latter body had to be summoned every three years and the
Council was responsible to it for its administration. In addition
declarations of war and peace and any alteration in the coinage
needed its approval. This period of Parliamentary government
in Sweden lasted until 1772 (when Gustavus III restored the
power of the Crown) and it has become notorious for fierce party
strife which gave foreign governments the opportunity of inter-
fering in Sweden's affairs, an opportunity of which Russia in
particular was not slow to take advantage.

[36] PEACE IN THE BALTIC, 1719–21: THE END OF SWEDEN'S EMPIRE

With regard to the war, the death of Charles XII removed the
greatest obstacle to a pacification of the north, but the Swedes,
though desperate, were still not prepared to make peace at any
price. They fully realized, nevertheless, that they must come to
terms with at least some of their adversaries, but whom would
it serve them best to choose? Should they join Peter, ceding the
Baltic provinces in the hope of compensation elsewhere, or
should they join George I, sacrificing their German possessions
in return for the support of the British fleet against Russia?
The breach between the Czar and the King of England was now

wider than ever. The destruction of the Spanish fleet in 1718 meant that George had nothing to fear from Alberoni and his intrigues in the north, and he thus began working openly not only to separate Russia from her allies but also to build up a league aimed at restoring Sweden's eastern provinces and so prevent Russian domination of the Baltic which seemed imminent. Ever since the Mecklenburg crisis animosity towards Russia had been growing in Britain. This feeling was strengthened by the rapid development of Russian naval and commercial power, and wild schemes of conquest were attributed to the Czar. The main grievance was, of course, the fear that Russia would monopolize the supply of naval stores, and particularly of flax and hemp, practically all of which came from Russia or the Baltic states. The British Minister, Lord Carteret, who was sent to Sweden to conduct peace negotiations in July 1719 was instructed that Peter must not become the master of the Baltic and that this was:

a consideration of such importance to the commerce of Our subjects and even to their safety, which could not be so well provided for without the naval stores We draw from those ports, that you are to labour this point with the utmost dexterity and application.[5]

After extremely prolonged and complex negotiations George I and his envoys were successful in isolating Russia and bringing about peace between Sweden and the rest of her foes. The King was aided by the fact that Peter, endeavouring to bring the Swedish government to see reason, raided the Swedish coast in July 1719 burning and pillaging the countryside as far as the outskirts of Stockholm, causing widespread damage. As a result the Swedes promptly signed a preliminary agreement with George I, ceding to him the long-coveted provinces of Bremen and Verden, in return for a money grant and the help of the British fleet against Russia. Simultaneously George made an alliance with Prussia, at last forcing Frederick William I to take up a clear position, and Sweden was persuaded to cede to him the excellent Baltic port of Stettin together with the southern portion of Pomerania and the islands of Usedom and Wollin in return for a large sum. (Sweden kept the rest of Pomerania until 1814

5. Quoted by J. F. Chance, op. cit.

when she ceded it to Denmark, who in 1815 relinquished it to
Prussia.) The final treaties were signed between Sweden and
Hanover in November 1719 and between Sweden and Prussia
and Sweden and Great Britain in January 1720. It now remained
to settle matters between Sweden and Denmark. In October 1719
George I, after lengthy discussions, brought about an armistice;
but the Danes obstinately clung to excessive demands and it was
not until the following summer that Frederick IV was prevailed
upon to give way. By the Treaty of Fredricksborg (July 1720)
Denmark undertook not to aid the Czar against Sweden and to
restore all territory which she had seized from the latter. In return Sweden promised not to assist the Duke of Holstein in
Schleswig (the ducal portion of which was guaranteed to Denmark by England and France), and gave up her exemption from
the Sound dues. Two long-standing sources of bitterness between
the Scandinavian powers were therefore removed. Sweden, having made these sacrifices, now looked forward confidently to recovering her Baltic provinces with the support of the British fleet.

She was to be grievously disappointed. The British navy was
indeed ordered to act with the Swedes against Russia, but both
in 1720 and in 1721 it remained inactive while further raids of
devastation (one in each year) were carried out on the Swedish
coast. It had in fact become clear that Peter would never be
defeated unless land forces were also employed against him.
But George I was quite unable to persuade his allies to cooperate
in such an endeavour and Britain herself, amid the financial
crisis known as the South Sea Bubble, grew anxious for peace so
that the expensive Baltic squadron could be withdrawn. Sweden
was therefore left to secure the best terms she could when the
peace conference finally opened with Russia at Nystad in Finland
in April 1721. The British Minister Townshend wrote hopefully
to Admiral Norris of the consequences which might result from
the appearance that year of the British fleet:

three or four days sooner or later may be of the last consequence at
this critical juncture with regard to the obtaining a Peace in the
North.[6]

6. Quoted by J. F. Chance, op. cit.

THE BALTIC, 1721

But this last effort on Sweden's behalf was in vain. In August peace was signed: Sweden ceded Livonia, Estonia, Ingria and part of Carelia – all the coastline of the Gulf of Finland from Riga to Viborg. In return the Czar restored Finland, promised not to interfere in Sweden's internal affairs, and allowed her to import duty-free grain from Riga. Peter had finally won his 'window on the west'. He wrote to Prince Vasily Dolgoruky:

All students of science normally finish their course in seven years: our schooling has lasted three times as long, but, praise God, it has all ended so well that it could not be better.[7]

At celebrations in St Petersburg the Czar was proclaimed: 'Father of the Fatherland, Peter the Great, Emperor of all Russia'.

The wheel of fortune had come full circle. Having seized supremacy of the Baltic from Denmark and thwarted the ambitions of Poland, Russia and Prussia, it was now Sweden's turn to be shorn of her possessions, to become once again a minor power. But, in retaining the Scanian provinces as well as the lands she had won from Norway, Sweden was considerably stronger both economically and territorially than she had been at the opening of the seventeenth century. Thus her old rival, Denmark, did not regain control of both sides of the Sound and was henceforth equally unable to make a bid to dominate the Baltic. In fact the settlement of 1720, which lasted until the Napoleonic wars, established a very even balance between the two Scandinavian powers while the actual boundaries of Denmark, Norway and Sweden have remained until the present day. At last an end had been put to the fierce conflicts between them for *dominium maris baltici*, a struggle which had continued for nearly two centuries and which only resulted in the eclipse of both. Neither would ever again aspire to play a major part in international affairs; and both needed a long period of peace to recover from the recent wars. In particular, it is estimated that Sweden lost 30 per cent of her man power during the Great Northern War; agriculture had declined seriously and trade was almost at a standstill. It

7. Quoted by Ian Grey, op. cit. p. 378.

was the end of an epoch in her history: the period of military greatness had closed for ever.

The collapse of Sweden's Baltic empire was inevitable. With no homogeneity of race, religion or culture, communications by sea often difficult, and with no natural frontiers, it depended ultimately upon military and naval power on a large scale, an enormous burden for a country sparsely populated and with few resources; moreover, it was a constant source of envy to Sweden's neighbours. The wonder is that it endured as long as it did. The main reasons for this were first a succession of extraordinary monarchs, and secondly the fact that for many years no power in the north was strong enough to challenge the hegemony of the Swedes while in the later period the French wars and the Turkish threat diverted attention from the Baltic. But sooner or later the Swedish empire was bound to fall and Charles XII was responsible for it being sooner rather than later. Determined not to yield an inch, he rejected on several occasions reasonable offers of alliance and of peace, and in the end nothing except Finland could be rescued from the collapsing Swedish empire. Upon its ruins arose two new powers, Prussia and Russia, the latter to be Sweden's heir to supremacy in the Baltic. As B. H. Sumner aptly puts it:

> Sweden had fallen; Russia more than took her place.[8]

[37] RUSSIA THE STRONGEST POWER IN THE NORTH

A major readjustment in the Baltic balance of power had therefore taken place once more; but this time it was with greater suddenness and drama than ever before in the struggle for supremacy. Russia, only two decades earlier almost entirely ignored

8. B. H. Sumner, *Peter the Great and the Emergence of Russia*, English University Press (London, 1951).

by the rest of Europe, was now the most formidable state in the
north. The most striking feature of this development was the
growth of Russian naval power. In 1710 there were no Russian
battleships in the Baltic but in 1722 Peter had more men-of-war
than either Denmark or Sweden, the two former Baltic sea-
powers, both having lost about half their strength during the war.
Furthermore this expansion took place despite the great hostility
and ignorance of the Russian people, the loss of Azof and the
nascent Black Sea fleet, and constant opposition from the
Swedish navy, originally, of course, far stronger. By the end of
Peter's reign (1725) the Russian fleet consisted of 48 ships of the
line and nearly 800 galleys, and it maintained its position of
superiority in the Baltic until the rise of the German navy at the
end of the nineteenth century. This was of no small significance
to the maritime powers and they found themselves equally affected
by the remarkable expansion which took place in Russian Baltic
trade. Peter successfully diverted the merchants of western Europe,
who were bound for Russia, from the White Sea routes to the
ports in the Baltic and the majority of this trade went via St
Petersburg, a rapidly growing city symbolizing the Czar's
achievements and Russia's new position within Europe. Thus in
1710 153 ships from the west called at Archangel, but in 1725
914 ships arrived in the Russian Baltic ports. Some indication of
the importance of Russian commerce in the Baltic may be gauged
from the fact that when the Sound dues were abolished in 1857
Russian trade accounted for nearly one third of the total, only a
little less than that of Great Britain.

Denmark and Sweden soon felt the full weight of Russia's
newly found power. The Czar demanded exemption from the
Sound dues and he espoused the cause of the Duke of Holstein,
thus threatening Frederick IV in his possession of Schleswig,
and Frederick I in his possession of the Swedish crown. Indeed,
in spite of Peter's undertaking at Nystad, Russian influence in
Sweden's internal affairs steadily grew, bribery being extensively
practised among the members of the Riksdag. By signing an
offensive and defensive alliance with Russia in 1724 the Swedes
vainly hoped that they would recover some of their lost territories,

and a conciliatory policy towards Russia was pursued for the next sixteen years. But anti-Russian feeling remained strong and war was once more declared on Russia in 1741 with disastrous results: still more of Finland was lost. Thus the Swedes were forced to face the fact that their losses were permanent and that they were too weak to challenge Russia with any hope of success.

If Russia influenced the affairs of Sweden, she dominated those of Poland. When Augustus II, attempting to establish himself as an absolute monarch, provoked the violently hostile nobles to form the 'Confederation of Tarnogrod' against his Saxon army, it was the Czar's ambassador who settled the dispute in 1717 by an agreement which, among other things, limited the Polish army to the ludicrous figure of 24,000. The following year Russian troops occupied Courland and thus all that remained of Poland's Baltic sea-board, so extensive in 1600, was West Prussia, inevitably the object of Hohenzollern ambition. When Augustus sought to free himself from his dependence upon Peter by allying with the Emperor and Great Britain in 1719, the Poles refused to agree to the treaty, determined not to be drawn into any further wars. A great opportunity was lost and henceforth Peter and his successors interfered with increasing boldness in Poland's internal affairs. In 1720 the Czar signed a treaty with Frederick William I by which they aimed at maintaining Poland's political disorder in their own interests; and this was only the first of many similar agreements. Four years later, after a group of Protestants had been persecuted at Thorn, Russia and Prussia guaranteed each other's right to protect the Orthodox and Protestant minorities in Roman Catholic Poland, and thus provided themselves with an excellent excuse for future meddling. Economically and culturally Poland's decline continued while only four Diets ran their course under Augustus II, and only one under his son. The latter was forced upon the Poles by Russia in 1733, despite the general preference for Stanislas Leszczynski; 1764 saw Catherine the Great install as king one of her former lovers, Stanislas Poniatowski. Clearly dismemberment was not far distant.

Nor was Peter's influence confined to the Baltic and Poland. His Holstein and Mecklenburg schemes, his efforts to conclude

a marriage alliance with France, all aroused trepidation among
the powers of Europe. In short not only was the Baltic equilibrium radically altered but the European balance of power likewise. Diplomatic contact had been established between Russia
and the foremost European powers; she was now a naval and
military power of the first importance and henceforth she would
play a major part in the affairs of Europe. This is the measure
of Peter the Great's achievement in his western policy. Despite
the fact that he was succeeded by a line of weak rulers, he had
permanently revolutionized his country's international position.
Moreover he had cooperated both in the Baltic and in Poland
with another state new to European power politics – Prussia.
But, although Frederick William I had been successful in gaining
the long-coveted Baltic port of Stettin on the Oder, he lacked
ability in the field of diplomacy and it was not until the War of
the Austrian Succession (1740–8) that Prussia's full strength
became apparent. Nevertheless he bequeathed on his death in
1740 a state and an army developed to a pitch of extreme efficiency, which proved a devastating weapon in the hands of his
son, Frederick the Great. In many of the new problems facing
eighteenth-century Europe – the struggle for power in Germany,
the partition of Poland, the question of European Turkey – the
voices of Russia and Prussia were to be decisive.

Principal Events of the Great Northern War, 1700—21

1700
Sweden attacked by Danes, Russians and Saxons
8 August. Peace of Traventhal: Charles XII subdues Denmark
20 November. Battle of Narva: Charles defeats Russians

1701
June. Charles saves Riga

1702
May. Charles captures Warsaw
July. Battle of Clissow: Charles defeats Saxons and Poles. Charles
  captures Cracow

1703
Russians capture Ingria
April. Battle of Pultusk: Charles defeats Saxons
October. Charles captures Thorn

1704
Russians capture Dorpat and Narva
January. Poles renounce Augustus in favour of Charles's nominee
  Stanislas Leczczynski
July. Stanislas Leczczynski elected to Polish throne

1705
September. Stanislas crowned

1706
3 February. Swedish victory over Saxons at Fraustadt
September. Treaty of Altranstädt: final humiliation of Augustus

1707
April. Meeting between Charles and Marlborough
August. Charles marches towards Russia

1708
30 June. Swedes defeat Russians at Holovzin
September. Swedes defeated by Russians at Lesnaya
October. Fugitive Mazeppa arrives in Swedish camp
November. Cossack capital sacked by Russians

1708–9
Severe winter in Ukraine

1709
May. Charles besieges Poltava
28 June. Battle of Poltava: Swedes defeated and Charles takes
    refuge in Turkey
November. Denmark invades Scania

1710
Danes defeated by Swedes at Hälsingborg
Russia conquers remaining Swedish Baltic territories
Turkey declares war on Russia

1711
July. Peter narrowly escapes disaster at the Pruth

1712
New Swedish army lands in Germany where Russians, Danes and
    Saxons are attacking Swedish possessions
Elector of Hanover occupies Verden

1713
Swedish army surrenders. Prussia occupies Stettin

1714
July. Russian naval victory off Cape Hango. Peter conquers
    Finland
August. Elector of Hanover becomes King of England
November. Charles arrives in Stralsund

1715
January. Hanover, Denmark and Prussia partition Sweden's
    German possessions

February. British fleet sent to the Baltic
April. Prussia declares war on Sweden
October. Hanover declares war on Sweden
November. Fall of Stralsund

1716
Short-lived attack on Norway by Charles
Projected Russo-Danish attack on Scania falls through

1717
Charles's chief minister Görtz, suspected of intriguing with
    Jacobites, arrested in Netherlands
Large British fleet to Baltic

1718
Discussions between Sweden and Russia on the Åland Islands
30 November. Charles killed during second Norwegian campaign

1719
May. Ulrica Eleonora crowned Queen of Sweden. Later abdicates
    in favour of her husband, Frederick of Hesse
November. Sweden cedes Bremen and Verden to Hanover

1720
January. Sweden cedes Stettin and part of Pomerania to Prussia
July. Peace of Fredricksborg between Sweden and Denmark

1721
August. Peace of Nystad: Sweden cedes Baltic provinces to Russia

Further Reading

J. F. CHANCE, *George I and the Northern War*. Smith, Elder (London, 1909).

M. S. ANDERSON, *Britain's Discovery of Russia 1553–1815*. Macmillan (London, 1956).

FRANS BENGTSSON, *The Life of Charles XII, King of Sweden, 1697–1718*. Macmillan (London, 1960).

R. NISBET BAIN, *Charles XII*. Putnam (New York and London, 1895).

M. SRIGLEY, 'The Death of Charles XII of Sweden'. *History Today* December (1963).

IAN GREY, *Peter the Great, Emperor of All Russia*. Hodder (London, 1962).

VASILI KLYUCHEVSKY, *Peter the Great*. Macmillan (London, 1958).

B. H. SUMNER, *Peter the Great and the Emergence of Russia*. English Universities Press (London, 1951).

B. H. SUMNER, 'Peter the Great'. *History* (March 1947).

IAN GREY, 'Peter the Great and the Creation of the Russian Navy'. *History Today* (September 1961).

L. R. LEWITTER, 'Mazeppa'. *History Today* (September 1957).

RAGNHILD MARIE HATTON, *Charles XII of Sweden*. Weidenfeld and Nicolson (London, 1968).

See also pages 44–5.

PART VIII
Reform in Russia and Prussia

INTRODUCTION

Our picture of the changing relationships of the Baltic states is not quite complete. Russia and Prussia could not have emerged as formidable powers in the eighteenth century without the intensive internal reorganization which was carried out in those countries by Peter I (1689–1725) and Frederick William I (1713–40) respectively. The latter's activities extend somewhat beyond our period but in fact the decade 1713–23 was the most significant in the reform of Prussia and almost identical with the years of reconstruction in Russia.

In many respects Peter and Frederick William worked along parallel lines; their countries were economically backward and lacked the strength which the states of the west derived from the middle classes; in both the administrative system was only barely centralized. Above all these two rulers were keenly aware of the limitations of their armed forces: thus the programme of reform in Russia and Prussia was essentially military and left a lasting impression upon the state. Peter and Frederick William were among the first monarchs to wear uniform regularly and they both took infinite care with every detail of army management and training. Upon their armies they lavished about two-thirds of their hard-won revenue, and the increasing military requirements of the state necessitated large-scale economic and administrative improvements in Russia and Prussia in order to stimulate production and increase the yield of taxation. In both countries

the landowning class was found to be indispensable in this programme, to officer the army and to provide the chief administrators (although both monarchs, especially Frederick William,
made use of the non-noble and the foreigner). After considerable
opposition Peter and Frederick William compelled the nobility
to give life-long service to the state in these capacities. Neither,
therefore, dared to interfere with the social privileges of the
nobles, and, as pressure from the state grew, the burdens of the
peasants increased. Far-reaching reforms of the administration
were carried out; the system of fiscals (spies for the government
against corruption) was extended in Prussia and adopted in
Russia; every available source of revenue was exploited. Skilled
workmen and manufacturers from abroad were given inducements and privileges (especially religious freedom) to build up
industry, while the state organized guilds, set up factories and
regulated trade in order to encourage exports and prohibit
imports. Efforts, though not very successful, were made in both
countries to promote primary education, and the Church was
carefully supervised by the government. Each monarch was
completely devoted to the welfare of his country and regarded
himself as the first servant of the state: each worked excessive
hours (and expected his subordinates to do likewise); upon
him alone depended the whole burden of the administrative
machine, and upon his initiative depended all projects of reform.
They both travelled constantly throughout their dominions,
supervising, inspecting, compelling, punishing. Their word was
law and they harshly enforced their will. It is notorious that Peter
was responsible for the death in 1718 of his unsatisfactory heir,
Alexis, and that Frederick William threatened his son, the
future Frederick the Great, with execution after he had attempted
to flee from his father's tyranny.

But, despite numerous similarities both of temperament and
policy, the personalities of these two rulers, the traditions of their
peoples and the conditions of their states, naturally varied enormously. In particular the vast distances within Russia and the
extreme backwardness of the official classes meant that Peter,
himself too impetuous, was less successful than Frederick William

in forging a fully centralized, efficient, administration. On the other hand, the Czar's predecessors had failed to lay foundations as firm as those built in Prussia by Frederick William's famous grandfather. the Great Elector. Moreover, in contrast to Frederick William, Peter succeeded in constructing a powerful fleet from nothing and pursued a dynamic foreign policy in a reign which saw only one completely peaceful year. He was indeed a many-sided genius, far less narrow than Frederick William (or, for that matter, Charles XII). The Prussian made little use of Stettin, acquired at last in 1721, and had small understanding of diplomacy. Furthermore, after the signing of peace at Nystad he did not risk his beautiful army in actual warfare.

[38] THE REFORMS OF PETER THE GREAT

It has been pointed out many times that Peter the Great did not devise a single, large-scale, systematic programme of reform which he launched all of a piece upon his backward nation. For years he was fully occupied with the Swedish and Turkish wars and had little time for detailed planning even if he had so desired. In fact reform was originally forced upon him by urgent military and financial needs: indeed Klyuchevsky argues that Peter became a reformer, as it were, by accident. As a result, the Czar's early measures were often contradictory, set on foot in fits and starts and hastily improvised according to the exigencies of the moment. But after Poltava (1709), with the threat of invasion removed, Peter's reforming activities became more widespread, and from about 1716, when the northern war was clearly won, they showed increasing thought and consistency. Much of the earlier work was revised and clarified; legislation became more complicated and was often prefaced by lengthy explanations of policy; and Peter revealed a growing concern with the aims and purposes of government based upon the rule of law.

In the early years he was primarily engaged in building up the armed forces, in stimulating industry, particularly cloth and munitions, and in discovering expanding sources of revenue. He needed men trained in military and industrial skills and, as time passed, the old administrative machine, unable to cope with the new programme, required drastic overhaul. A competent official class was indispensable to carry out these policies and thus Peter made great efforts to provide facilities for the education and training of the Russian nobility. Gradually every aspect of national life felt the force of his will and towards the end of his reign, as the pressures of war eased, he found time to devote to more liberal and cultural matters. But he was all the time working against the tremendous indifference, ignorance and widespread corruption, that pervaded all levels of Russian life. This, together with frequent errors of judgment on Peter's part, made certain that confusion rather than efficiency remained in many departments of Russian life even after the Czar's very real achievements. A contemporary writer, Pososhkov, aptly commented:

The Czar pulls uphill alone with the strength of ten, but millions pull downhill.

From the reconstruction of Russia's defensive system, then, all other reforms stemmed; however it must not be forgotten when studying these developments that the Czar pursued many of his numerous schemes simultaneously and in no particular order. Reference has already been made to Peter's naval and military achievements and he can be accurately described not only as the founder of the Russian navy, but also as the creator of a modern standing army, established on the western model which, by his death, numbered over 200,000 men. Henceforth Russia was a military power of first rank in Europe despite a certain diminishing of her armed strength under Peter's immediate successors. But, by quartering the new army on the population, by imposing heavy taxation for its upkeep as well as for that of the navy, and by enforcing conscription for both forces, Peter added greatly to the burdens of the peasants. As for the landowners, military service for life was to be their first duty, passing through the ranks to become officers either in the army, or in the more unpopular navy. Actually a post in the civil administration was the most attractive form of service as it presented opportunity for financial rewards and involved less hardship, but Peter insisted that only one-third of each noble family should enter the bureaucracy: the rest were thus reserved for the armed forces.

War stimulated Russia's economy; Peter set himself to develop the resources and trade of his realm and so increase her wealth. Initially, of course, he was concerned with military needs and thus particularly with building up the nascent iron industry. No less than fifty-two new iron works were established during his reign, thirteen of which were situated in the Urals, a newly discovered rich source of iron and copper, soon to be the most important industrial area in the country. By 1716 Russia was not only producing all the iron necessary to supply her own army and navy, but was exporting some to Britain. Fifty years later she was the greatest producer of iron in Europe, bearing witness to Peter's lasting contribution in this field. Simultaneously with the progress made towards self-sufficiency in iron, the Czar saw to it that Russia should no longer be so dependent upon foreign cloth (mainly used for the army) by setting up fifteen new textile factories which by 1725 drastically reduced imports of woollen goods. In addition new saw mills were established to improve the supply of timber, while the sail-cloth, rope and leather industries were made more productive. Practically all the new enterprises which were promoted in Russia before Poltava were set up by the state with the requirements of the armed forces in mind; but from 1710 onwards other more peaceful undertakings such as china, glass, paper, silk, velvet and stockings increased in number. However, Peter's greatest difficulty was the lack of a thriving middle class which possessed sufficient initiative and capital to manage these matters itself. Hoping to create such a class, Peter gave the few manufacturers and industrialists in Russia exceptional privileges, including a large measure of self-government over the towns. He compelled them to form companies which were not only exempted from taxes and permitted to purchase raw materials free of duty, but which received generous financial assistance. After 1710 Peter handed over certain state factories to private enterprise while in 1724 he imposed a prohibitive tariff on competitive foreign goods. But in general the new companies failed, on the one hand through incompetent management and lack of initiative, and on the other through excessive government compulsion and regulation. Moreover Peter was constantly grappling with the problem of the lack of skilled craftsmen: many parties of Russians were sent abroad for training and foreigners were encouraged to settle in Russia in an effort to remedy this deficiency. As for the labour supply, the Czar introduced the iniquitous practice of drafting huge numbers of peasants to the mines and factories and in 1721 he went so far as to allow the industrialists to purchase serfs (hitherto an exclusive privilege of the nobility). On the whole, despite the failure of many projects, Peter's achievements in promoting Russian industry were remarkable, not only during his own life time, but also as foundations for the future economic expansion of the nation. Likewise Russian exports via the Baltic ports doubled and redoubled in the most striking manner, and by 1725 exports to the rest of Europe were twice the value of imports.

As regards agriculture, little was done, though efforts were made to compel the peasants to reap with the scythe rather than the sickle and, in the northern provinces, to produce more hemp and flax. Great impetus, however, was given to Russia's system of communications, especially to the building of canals. In 1708 the canal linking the Volga and the Neva was opened, while in 1718, with appalling wastage of peasant labour, work began on a canal to bypass lake Ladoga, prone to severe storms. Peter's vision of a system of waterways linking the White, Baltic, Caspian and Black Seas was not realized until the next century, but he had prepared the way for his successors.

Waging almost continuous war, Peter needed enormous supplies of ready money and as none was raised by loans either domestic or foreign, the whole burden fell upon the taxpaying community of one generation. He resorted to every expedient to increase the revenue: in 1701 most of the great wealth of the Church was diverted to the treasury; the coinage was debased;

state monopolies, already on potash, glue and alcohol, were extended to chalk, pitch, oak coffins, chessmen, playing cards and,
most injurious of all, salt. With the aid of 'revenue-finders',
whose job it was to discover new sources of income, taxes were
placed on beards, windows, cellars, mills, bridges, private baths,
boats, hats, shoes and even pettier items such as stovepipes,
beehives, melons and cucumbers. A stamp duty was introduced;
Old Believers were forced to pay double taxes, and the
freemen of the northern lands were ordered to pay to the state
those dues which other peasants paid to their lords. But,
despite this ingenuity, revenue actually declined between 1703
and 1710. In particular, it was discovered that the main direct
tax levied upon households was being widely evaded by the
peasants who were grouping themselves into very large households. Thus after much thought Peter decided, on returning from
a visit to Paris, to introduce the French system of a poll-tax.
It was to be levied upon all males (except the nobles and clergy),
including children and old men, and upon all groups such as
beggars, children of priests, monastery servants and slaves, who
had hitherto not been liable for tax. The new census returns were
largely falsified and in fact Peter died before he could see the
final results. But in 1724 when the tax was levied for the first
time it produced more than half the income of the state and remained the most important tax in Russia until the end of the
century. At the end of Peter's reign the revenue was two and a
half times the level of 1680 but the peasant community was
severely overstrained. Not only were the state taxes trebled and
military conscription harshly enforced during this period, but
the serfs had heavy obligations to their masters and were forced
also to labour in the mines and factories, to build canals and the
new capital St Petersburg.

The old Muscovite central government, consisting of the jumble
of departments known as the *prikazy*, and the corrupt, inefficient,
Duma of Boyars (the council of magnates), was quite unable to
administer Peter's unending demands for men, money and
equipment; while in the provinces the situation was little better.
In particular the Czar was anxious to eliminate waste and corrup-

tion from the financial system. In 1708 the position was so serious that he decided to bypass the confusion at the centre and divide the country into eight enormous 'governments' in the hope that the local governors, endowed with very wide powers, would be more successful in financing and provisioning the army. The Duma had by then disappeared and Peter worked alone with no central body capable of coordinating and supervising affairs but merely with a chancery to record his decrees. Thus in 1711 he established a Senate of nine members to act as the government while he was absent fighting the Turks, but on his return he retained it permanently. It acted as a link with the provinces and as a high court of appeal; it prepared legislation and, most important, administered finance.

But it soon became increasingly obvious that the Senate was overworked: its members were constantly at loggerheads and it was quite unable to keep account of government receipts and expenditure. It was this failure which led Peter to introduce in 1718, after consulting foreign advisers, a system of colleges based on the Swedish model which would take the place of the *prikazy*. The nine original colleges were for Foreign Affairs, Commerce, Industry, Justice, War, Admiralty, State Revenue, State Expenditure, and the coordination of finances. This was a much more rational allocation of responsibility and meant that the Senate was freed from routine administration to concentrate upon its legislative, judicial and supervisory functions. Each college had a president, a vice-president (usually a foreigner), four councillors and a clerical staff. Enormous difficulties had to be faced, in particular the scarcity of experienced foreigners who were needed to explain the technicalities of the new system to the Russians, and the language barrier between the nationalities. In the end the college presidents tended to become all-powerful, and confusion and lack of coordination in the administration was by no means eradicated. Nevertheless it is true to say that in 1725 the central government was strikingly more efficient than it had been before Peter's time. Moreover the colleges, though undergoing many readjustments, remained intact for a century, while the Senate, equally modified, was not finally abolished until 1917.

The Czar waged a constant war against the great Russian evils of maladministration and corruption which were to be found even among the Senators themselves. The hated system of fiscals had been instituted throughout the country and, in fact, everyone was expected to act as a spy for the government. As the successful informer was rewarded with the wrong-doer's property, denouncing was widespread, although innumerable false accusations were made. In 1722 Peter set up a very powerful official, the Procurator-General, who was to act as the Czar's 'eye' in the Senate and preside over its meetings. He had his own staff of procurators attached to each college, and the fiscals were also subordinated to his authority.

Administration in the provinces was also overhauled, though with far less success, by a series of measures which revealed considerable lack of forethought. After 1708 various experiments were made: in 1713 boards of councillors were set up to assist each provincial governor; in 1715 the huge provinces were subdivided, and each district had its own board. But in 1719 this system was abandoned and Russia was divided into fifty provinces, once more under *voivodes*. However, justice (which was extremely slow and complex, for Peter did not succeed in his intention of re-codifying the law) was to be administered separately under the College of Justice. Moreover in 1724 the new regimental districts into which Peter had divided the country for the purposes of billeting the army, and which cut across the provinces, were made responsible for collecting the poll tax and for administering conscription. The new arrangements were far too complicated and in many respects ran contrary to Russian custom: they were scrapped soon after Peter's death.

In municipal affairs the Czar had greater success though he did not realize his ambition of creating a strong middle class such as he had seen in the west. In 1721 the merchants, manufacturers and skilled workers were formed into two guilds based on the system operating in Riga and Reval. In each town the wealthier citizens were elected to the Board of Magistracy which controlled municipal government and which was subordinated to the Chief Magistracy in St Petersburg. But the latter soon dominated the provincial towns and largely prevented the growth of municipal independence.

Taken as a whole, Peter had achieved much in reconstructing Russia's administrative machine despite great haste and confusion and the persistence of many deficiencies only too clearly described by Klyuchevsky. In particular the Czar was unable to root out the widespread extortion and lawlessness, although, by means of savage punishment, he did effect some improvement. In his last years he relied more and more upon his loyal Guards officers (who were to become enormously powerful during the following weak reigns) to carry out his will against those in authority. Unfortunately this atmosphere of compulsion was hardly conducive to the growth of enterprise and public-spiritedness which Peter hoped to foster.

The Church was not spared from the Czar's reforming activities although he did not interfere with matters of dogma. Despite his frequent mocking of the Russian Orthodox hierarchy and the ritual it observed, Peter was not fundamentally irreligious. But he was determined that the Patriarchate, always a potential source of opposition, should be subordinated to the authority of the state. Thus in 1700 when Patriarch Adrian died, his office was left vacant. Eventually in 1721 it was abolished altogether and in its place as head of the Church was established the 'Holy Governing Synod'. This was a board of bishops, similar to a college, with its own Chief Procurator as the representative of the Czar. In all essentials the Synod remained in existence until 1917 when the Patriarchate was restored. Peter intended that education should be one of the primary aims of this new institution and no less than forty-six diocesan schools for the training of priests were established and were teaching to a liberal curriculum by his death in 1725. In addition the Czar ordered that monastic discipline be more strictly enforced so that the numbers of monks and nuns, whom he regarded as unproductive, should be severely limited. The laity were fined for non-attendance at church which was practically the only source of dissemination for government decrees. Finally Peter initiated the beginnings in Russia of a more tolerant attitude towards people of different faiths: the

Old Believers who were often a hardworking section of the community (particularly in the iron-producing Olonets region), the Lutherans in the Baltic provinces, Roman Catholics and even Jesuits, were permitted freedom to worship.

During Peter's reign a far heavier burden of service was imposed upon the different classes than they had been accustomed to in the seventeenth century, and the whole structure of society was clarified and regularized as a result of his reforms. The landowning class was particularly affected: Peter succeeded in asserting the principle that every noble must be entered upon the service registers at the age of ten and failure to do so was severely punished. At fifteen the noble owed service to the state for life either in the army, the navy or the bureaucracy. In the hope of creating a supply of landless nobles Peter issued a decree in 1714 ordering that estates should be bequeathed to one son or relative but not, as was the Muscovite custom, divided between members of the family. This measure was not a success and was abandoned soon after the Czar's death. More significant was the 'table of ranks' which Peter instituted in 1722. All posts in the military and civil services were classified into fourteen parallel grades and everyone had to start at the bottom. All ranks in the army and navy and the top eight grades in the bureaucracy automatically carried with them the privileges of nobility. As a result, commoners and foreigners had an opportunity to enter the ranks of the aristocracy and birth gave place to merit in the social scale. Peter insisted that it was the duty of every noble to be educated and, if necessary, to travel abroad and study subjects such as economics, languages and the art of war to equip himself for state service. At home, teachers from the School of Mathematics, established in 1701, were sent into the provinces to teach young nobles between the ages of ten and fifteen, but attendance was poor. Thus in 1714 the Czar decided upon compulsion and decreed that unless a noble could produce a certificate proving that he had received such an education he should be forbidden to marry. This measure was quite ineffective and two years later Peter revoked it. He then ordered, more successfully, that the children of the landowners should attend one of the three new schools he had established in St Petersburg, the Naval, Military and Engineering Academies. Nor was this all: the nobles were also expected to adopt western dress and customs, to entertain each other in social gatherings, and to follow the social rules which were set down in the first Russian guide to etiquette that Peter had introduced. However, in general, compulsory state service was unpopular with the upper class, particularly with the great nobles and, after the Czar's death, they succeeded in reducing their obligations until in 1762 they were freed completely from any legal duty to serve. Nevertheless they continued to dominate civil and military affairs and after Peter's time entry into the class became increasingly difficult.

Peter devoted much attention to the merchant classes. He endeavoured to promote initiative and self-government in the towns and he set up schools run by the admiralty, later replaced by garrison schools, to educate the sons of the merchants and priests. But, again, these efforts met with little response.

The peasants, in contrast to the other classes, received no benefits, only weightier burdens. The Czar was, indeed, aware of their misery, and he did something to encourage the establishment of almshouses, orphanages and hospitals and ordered that serfs should not be sold separately from their families. But serfdom to him was a necessary evil, and the increased demands of the state for money, men and labour, together with the desire of the landowners for more serfs, strictly under their control, meant that the majority of peasants were bound more closely to their masters while bondage was extended to include groups which had hitherto escaped. The demands in particular of the tax-collectors and recruiting officers occasioned great distress: agrarian disturbances and peasant flight were frequent. Those who escaped were mercilessly hunted down and in 1722 Peter ordered that no serf could leave his master's estate without written permission, in other words, a passport. During the eighteenth century, while other European states were moving towards greater freedom for the individual, the situation of the peasants in Russia grew worse and the gulf between the classes even wider: the ultimate result was revolution.

Until Peter's time all matters of learning were in the hands of the Church and, despite the apathy with which the Czar had to contend in his efforts to combat ignorance, a great stimulus was given to lay education during his reign. Apart from those educational institutions already mentioned, a medical school was opened in 1706 and at the time of his death Peter was planning the establishment of the Academy of Sciences (set up in 1726), later to become one of the most important centres for higher learning and research in Russia. Twice as many books were printed in Russia during Peter's reign as in the whole of the seventeenth century and a large proportion of them were, for the first time, secular. Admittedly they were mostly either government decrees and military manuals, or books on such technical subjects as arithmetic, astronomy and geography; but there were, too, some works of history. Few of these publications were sold but a significant start had been made in spreading learning. Moreover in 1707 the Czar initiated a very important reform: the Russian alphabet was simplified and made less cumbersome. Peter himself built up a great library with books on a wide range of subjects and, as time passed, he showed increasing interest in cultural matters. Russians were sent abroad to study architecture and painting, while foreign artists were encouraged to come to Russia. St Petersburg and the Czar's new palaces were laid out in the western style; in particular, the palace of Peterhof, eighteen miles from St Petersburg, was based upon Versailles and filled with pictures and statues bought abroad.

The impact of Peter the Great upon the development of Russia can be fairly described as revolutionary. It is true that much of his work was superficial, ill-thought out, and only lasted as long as his life time. But, despite the inevitable decline which occurred when his vigorous personal rule ended in 1725, most of the main essentials survived the succession of weak rulers which followed him. Peter acted upon Muscovy, comments B. H. Sumner, as 'a peasant hitting his horse with his fist', and it has been estimated that, without Peter, Russia would have taken another century to reach a comparable stage in her development, always providing, of course, she escaped the dangers of foreign invasion and internal dissension. There is, indeed, much to censure in Peter's conduct, particularly his barbaric cruelty and his endless demands for sacrifices from his people; but it is doubtful whether any man could have accomplished more than he did with the material he had at his disposal. The great tragedy was the lack of a suitable heir to carry on his work. Alexis, Peter's son by his first wife, was out of sympathy with his father's radical changes and, temperamentally a dreamer, somewhat lazy and with little aptitude either for military leadership or administration, he was a great disappointment to his exceptionally energetic and resourceful father. Inevitably, Alexis became the centre of opposition hopes, although he was in no way the leader of a rebellion against Peter. But the latter feared, probably justifiably, that much of his work, particularly that of building up the armed forces, would be nullified if Alexis succeeded and it was presumably the Czar's inhuman belief that the good of the state required the extinction of his son. In terror of his father, Alexis fled to the Emperor for protection, but, being promised forgiveness, he was persuaded to return to Russia where he and his friends found themselves subjected to a ferocious inquisition. Finally, after torture, Alexis died in 1718, and his baby son (also Peter) was the only male survivor of the Romanov line on the death of the Czar in 1725. Consequently Peter's second wife, the Livonian peasant girl Catherine, who had made an eminently suitable partner for him, succeeded as Empress with the help of the devoted Guards.

[39] THE REFORMS OF FREDERICK WILLIAM I

In Brandenburg-Prussia the Great Elector had been succeeded in 1688 by his son, the Elector Frederick III, soon to achieve his life-long ambition and become King in Prussia (1701). Despite the fact that West Prussia was not part of his domains, he was actually known as Frederick I, King *of* Prussia, and this title was rapidly applied to all his lands. Indeed it became a unifying factor and the names 'Royal Prussian Army' and 'Royal Prussian Administration' were soon commonly in use. At this time titles and rank were greatly valued and undoubtedly Frederick I had rendered his country a considerable service; the kingship was an important element in the growth of Prussia's prestige and influence in Europe and an inspiration to succeeding Hohenzollern rulers. Moreover, although Frederick I lacked the strength of character and the ability of his father and his son, his reign was not without significance. The army continued to increase; canals were built; immigration was encouraged; and Frederick I succeeded in exempting all his territories from appeal to the imperial courts. Above all, ably supported by his wife, Sophia Charlotte of Hanover, the first Prussian king was a patron of the arts, a more attractive and ultimately more worthwhile preoccupation, it can be argued, than that which later absorbed his son. Berlin, greatly improved, became a true capital city and a flourishing centre of culture, while many notable men were attracted to the increasingly splendid court. In 1696 the Academy of Arts was founded and four years later the Academy of Sciences was established, with Leibnitz as its first president. Most important was the foundation of the University of Halle in 1694 which soon developed into a very enlightened, progressive institution, and an important centre of Pietism. At Halle lectures were given in German instead of Latin; the study of Germanic law was encouraged; and the new subjects of history and science were studied.

But Frederick I's passion for display, his love of jewellery, and the enormous sums spent on the court in an attempt to emulate Versailles, resulted in a huge deficit. Furthermore, with the dismissal in 1697 of Danckelmann, the chief minister, who had largely followed in the footsteps of the Great Elector, the King relied upon grasping, corrupt favourites, in particular Wartenberg. Their incompetence and mismanagement led to a serious decline in the efficiency of the administration and to a deterioration in the economic and financial stituation, made worse by plague and famine. Ultimately an inquiry was instituted on the

initiative of the Crown Prince, Frederick William, and the
winter of 1710–11 saw the downfall of the favourites. Thus, even
before he became king, Frederick William had made his influence
felt upon Prussian affairs.

Frederick William I succeeded his father in 1713. He worked
excessive hours, personally attending to all matters of government with the utmost concern for detail, economy, punctuality
and discipline. In one of his first letters as king he wrote:

Tell the Prince of Anhalt [a distinguished Prussian General] that I am
the Finance Minister and the Field Marshal of the King of Prussia;
this work will keep the King of Prussia on his legs.

He reduced the expenses of the court to a minimum; ruthlessly
cut down salaries in both civil and military affairs and eradicated
every form of extravagance. He was a Calvinist, somewhat puri-
tanical, and ruled his family sternly, often giving way to furious
bouts of temper. His relations with his son, who in contrast to
Frederick William, was fond of poetry and music, were particularly embittered and the King harshly punished his heir when
he attempted to flee to England, forcing him to witness the
execution of his dearest friend. But towards the end of Frederick
William's life, matters improved and each came to recognize
the other's merits. From his subordinates, as from his son, the
King demanded utter subjection to his will and devotion to his
service. In a marginal note of October 1714 he wrote:

One must serve the King with life and limb, with goods and chattels,
with honour and conscience and surrender everything except salvation. The latter is reserved to God. But everything else must be mine.[1]

The Privy Council, which was the chief advisory body during
the reign of the Great Elector and while Danckelmann remained
in power under Frederick I, declined in importance and Frederick
William ruled absolutely from his 'cabinet', an institution which
bore no resemblance to that developing in England. In Prussia
the King worked privately, assisted by a number of secretaries
who soon became highly experienced in matters of government

1. Quoted by R. Dorwart, *The Administrative Reforms of Frederick William I
of Prussia*, Harvard University Press (Cambridge, Mass., 1953).

and who dealt with the correspondence through which Frederick William kept in touch with his various administrative departments. His aim was to create in Prussia a fully efficient, centralized administration, to increase the resources and revenue of the state and above all to build up a large powerful army. In particular he was determined that his country should never again be dependent upon foreign subsidies to maintain the armed forces. As early as 1711 Frederick William wrote of his father's ministers:

I can but laugh at the scoundrels; they say they will obtain land and people for the King with the pen; but I say it can be done only by the sword, otherwise he will get nothing.

In his instructions to his heir he repeated time and again sentiments of a similar nature:

A formidable army and a fund large enough to make this army mobile in times of need can create great respect for you in the world, so that you can speak a word like the other powers.[2]

His preoccupation with the army earned him the title of *Soldatenkönig*, the Sergeant King. But the smiles of Europe, provoked in particular by Frederick William's constant drilling of his special regiment of giants, the Potsdam Grenadiers, were to disappear rapidly when the full strength of the new Prussian army was revealed by his son in 1740. Indeed, Frederick William I created an armed strength totally out of proportion to the size and manpower of Prussia. Numbering over 80,000 men in 1740, the army devoured 1 in 25 of the population as compared with 1 in 150 in France. Thus, while Prussia was tenth in Europe in population, she was fourth in military power. It is true that the King could not find sufficient men for his army within Prussia, and he obtained nearly a third of his soldiers abroad by means of hundreds of recruiting officers. In 1733 home recruitment was regularized when the country was divided into cantons of 5,000 households each, whose duty it was to supply young men to keep the local regiment up to strength. Skilled workers, however, were exempt, and even the peasants, provided they were present at the

2. Quoted by R. Ergang, *The Potsdam Führer. Frederick William I, Father of Prussian Militarism.* Columbia University Press (New York, 1941).

drills held in April and May, were allowed home for long periods
to help with the harvest. As for the officers, Frederick William
at first met with considerable opposition from the Junkers all of
whom he insisted owed military service to the state. The Great
Elector had made a start in inducing the territorial nobility to
enter the army, but service in a force which was still largely
mercenary in 1713, commanded, as often as not, by foreigners
and adventurers, was still not looked upon as an honour. Frederick
William soon changed this. He set a personal example, always
appearing in uniform, and he established a cadet corps in Berlin
in 1722 for the instruction and training of the sons of the nobility.
He held military service in greater esteem than civil service and
henceforth posts in the army carried with them the highest social
prestige and distinction. It was not long before a strong *esprit
de corps* and a high sense of duty to the state developed among
the privileged Prussian officer class, characteristics it was long
to retain. The general militarization of society was to be Frederick William's unique contribution to the history of the state.

Every care was taken and no expense spared with the army,
and particularly with the infantry. Frederick William supervised
all matters of organization, quarters, equipment, and discipline
which was extremely harsh. He issued regulations covering every
possible situation of war, far in advance of anything else in
Europe; he clothed his men in standardized uniforms of Prussian
blue, improved their guns and developed new tactics. Above all,
the manoeuvres and endless drills, often under the eagle eye of
the King, which led to rapidity of fire, precision and speed of
movement, brought the Prussian army to the height of efficiency
and made it the best fighting machine in Europe.

But, as always, the needs of so large an army demanded a
well-ordered administration to ensure a constant flow of money
and supplies. On his own initiative, Frederick William, between
1713 and 1723, completed the design of the Great Elector in such
a way as to create thoroughly centralized financial and military
institutions, staffed by able and loyal civil servants, and to build
up a full treasury and large surplus for war. He made the economy
more productive and increased the manpower of the state, all

such matters remaining under the control of the departments of war. The judicial system, however, did not benefit from similar intensive reforms. Frederick William was aware of its many deficiencies, but the overhaul of the administration of justice was not accomplished until his son's reign.

One important point, which must be clearly understood when examining Frederick William's fiscal and military reorganization, is that on becoming king in 1713 he inherited two separate sets of administrative institutions. One system dealt with civil affairs and was mainly concerned with administering the revenue gained from the old feudal dues and the very extensive domain lands belonging to the Crown. In fact the income flowing into the treasury for the domains was about half the total revenue of the state and was primarily devoted to the royal household and other matters of civil expenditure. The other group of officials, under the *Generalkriegskommissariat*, was evolved originally by the Great Elector to establish the state upon a strong military basis with efficient finances and a separate treasury, the *General-kriegskasse*. This department for war administered the revenue which was obtained from the excise tax on the towns (introduced by the Great Elector and extended by Frederick William) and from the much older tax upon the rural areas, known as the 'contribution' (a land tax, always specifically for military purposes). At the same time the *Generalkriegskommissariat* supervised general economic matters and especially the government's immigration policy.

The highest point in the development of both systems was reached under Frederick William I. In 1713 he consolidated the administration for the domains into a central body, the *General-finanzdirektorium*, or General Finance Directory, to which the Domain Chambers in the provinces and the Crown Bailiffs in the localities were subordinated. The latter leased the domain lands for a period of six years at a fixed rent, and kept the peace and administered justice in their areas. In 1712 the *General-kriegskommissariat*, hitherto an office held by one man, had been brought into line with other Prussian departments, and established on a collegiate basis. Under the new king centralization of the *Generalkriegskommissariat* went rapidly ahead and to it were subordinated the Provincial War Commissariats. Its local officers were the Rural Commissioners, or *Landräte*, in the countryside, and the very powerful Local Commissaries, or *Steuerräte*, who supervised the towns. Finally in 1714 Frederick William created an office to audit the accounts of both civil and military departments. It was dependent upon the King and equal in rank with both the *Generalfinanzdirektorium* and the *Generalkriegskommissariat*.

The Local Commissary was the most important subordinate official. By far the greatest proportion of military finance came from the excise tax and it was his primary duty to ensure that the maximum was raised efficiently and honestly. In general he saw to it that the area under his authority, perhaps one large town or a group of smaller ones, kept in line with government policy. His power rapidly grew until by 1740 self-government in the towns had largely disappeared and the old corrupt councils had been replaced by bodies of officials paid by the state, and under the strict control of the Local Commissary. It was he who initiated all improvements, supervised trade and industry, inspected food, regulated weights and measures, examined accounts and saw to the quartering of the army and the welfare of the troops.

The two parallel sets of institutions became increasingly centralized under their supreme bodies in Berlin and, as they grew in independence and power, each endeavoured to extend its jurisdiction and increase its authority. The resulting clashes at every level between the two rival administrations caused the King to write in 1721 to the General Finance Directory:

We have often observed that between your college and the electoral exchequer on the one hand and our general war commissariat on the other, differences have arisen over various matters which remain unsettled because neither college wishes to yield. So that all these difficulties may be abolished at one time we order herewith that the abovementioned colleges get together through deputies, discuss all those matters of disagreement and settle them by 1 January.[3]

3. Quoted by R. Dorwart, op. cit., p. 162.

But this did not solve the problem.

Finally the King decided to amalgamate the two systems although, fearing that the revenues for war might be squandered, he kept the treasuries separate. In his Instruction of January 1723 the evolution of the Prussian administration reached its climax. This document bears striking witness to the enormous detailed knowledge which the King possessed and the stress which he laid upon the economic welfare of the nation. It opened with the words:

After we found it to be highly necessary to abolish the *Generalkriegs-kommissariat* and the *Generalfinanzdirektorium* and to replace them with a *General-Ober-Finanz-Kriegs-und Domainendirektorium* (General Directory) and to give this college supervision of all affairs formerly in the competence of those two offices, we declare that we ourselves shall hold the Presidency over this Directory to add to it more lustre and authority and to show our special, constant and untiring attention to the affairs in its resort.[4]

Thus the new General Directory was to be responsible for the management of the finances, the military needs, and the general economic improvement of the whole of Brandenburg-Prussia. Its personnel consisted of five vice-presidents and fourteen councillors. It was divided into four departments each dealing upon a fixed day during the week with one or more general aspects of state administration, for example, coinage or the army, and with a certain geographical area, such as East Prussia or Minden. Every Saturday afternoon the war and domain treasuries were examined and any deficiency remedied. In March 1723 the auditing office was made subordinate to the General Directory. The King, by means of cabinet orders, was the supreme director of the system, and written reports of business from the various departments kept him in close contact with the central body. In each province the separate organs were amalgamated into the *Kriegs-und-Domainen-Kammer* (War and Domain Board). The local officials remained as before but now the Crown Bailiffs, Rural Commissioners and Local Commissaries were responsible to a single authority.

4. Quoted by R. Dorwart, op. cit., p. 200.

There were deficiencies: the division of labour at the centre remained confused throughout the century until the establishment of modern functional ministries by Stein in 1808; after 1740, the larger, wealthier state made it increasingly difficult for the King to keep in personal touch with all departments, and Frederick the Great had a tendency to bypass the General Directory with special commissions; finally, such a concentration of absolute power inevitably had serious dangers under less able monarchs. But there can be no doubt that by 1740 the government machine, as reformed by Frederick William I, was working extremely efficiently. From his cabinet, the King directed foreign affairs, through the institution known as the *Cabinetsministerium*; controlled justice, education and spiritual affairs through a department of the old Privy Council, the *Justizstaatsrat* and, most important, supervised financial, military and economic affairs through the General Directory. But Frederick William did not trust his officials. He extended the system of fiscals and subjected his civil servants to rigorous discipline. Their actions were perpetually scrutinized and they were always liable to sudden visits of inspection from the King himself during which the severest punishments were meted out to offenders. Nevertheless it is true to say that Frederick William succeeded in building up an efficient and, on the whole, an honest bureaucracy. It was recruited largely from the rising middle class, promptly paid and inculcated with a strong sense of duty. The State revenue was doubled during his reign and large reserves of bullion were collected for war. It was left to Frederick the Great to make use of the military and administrative strength which his father had hoarded.

Every effort was made to stimulate the backward economy of Prussia. Trade and industry were meticulously regulated; state monopolies increased; heavy duties were placed upon foreign goods, and the import of cloth, shoes and Polish grain were eventually completely forbidden. Home industries, such as beer, salt, paper, amber, sugar and, especially, cloth and leather, developed, while urban life increased. Berlin itself became a very important centre of woollen manufacture which was strictly controlled by the government and promoted in particular by the decree that the army should be dressed in Prussian manufactured cloth. Guilds were placed under state supervision, and journeymen, whose strikes had recently become troublesome, were subject to stringent control. Skilled workmen were forbidden to leave the country, while special inducements were offered to persuade skilled foreigners to come to Prussia. The traditional policy of encouraging immigration by state assistance continued throughout the reign and the most important group of settlers were about 20,000 refugees who fled from the bishopric of Salzburg in 1732. Unproductive elements were not tolerated; gypsies were expelled and beggars sent to workhouses.

The cultural life of Prussia was neglected, not unnaturally considering the personality and predilections of Frederick William, while his efforts to introduce compulsory elementary education in 1717 were largely unsuccessful. Furthermore, despite the initiative taken in naval affairs by the Great Elector, Frederick William I made no attempt to utilize the newly won port of Stettin or to make Prussia a Baltic sea-power. In fact the naval treasury which had been created in 1686 later became the basis for purchasing the Potsdam giants.

But Frederick William's contribution to the building of Brandenburg-Prussia was essential and far-reaching. He filled in the outline which had been drawn by the Great Elector and provided the means by which his son raised Prussia to the level of a great power. The traditions of absolutism, of devotion to the state, of bureaucratic efficiency and military power, which were established during Frederick William's reign, were to be of lasting significance throughout the future history of the state.

After the general pacification of the north in 1721 Prussia turned away from Baltic politics to concentrate upon her relationship with Austria and Poland, while Russia found herself involved once more with the problems of Poland and Turkey. Both became powers of first rank in the eighteenth century; both took their first steps to greatness in the Baltic.

Further Reading

B. H. SUMNER, *Peter the Great and the Emergence of Russia*. English Universities Press (London, 1951).

IAN GREY, *Peter the Great, Emperor of All Russia*. Hodder (London, 1962).

VASILI KLYUCHEVSKY, *Peter the Great*. Macmillan (London, 1958).

B. H. SUMNER, 'Peter the Great'. *History* (March 1947).

IAN GREY, 'Peter the Great and the Creation of the Russian Navy'. *History Today* (September 1961).

R. DORWART, *The Administrative Reforms of Frederick William I of Prussia*. Harvard University Press (Cambridge, Mass., 1953).

R. ERGANG, *The Potsdam Führer. Frederick William I, Father of Prussian Militarism*. Columbia University Press (New York, 1941).

See also pages 44–5.

Appendix I
Table of Contemporary Rulers of the Baltic States, 1600–1725

SWEDEN	DENMARK	POLAND	RUSSIA	BRANDEN-BURG-PRUSSIA
		Sigismund III 1587–1632		
	Christian IV 1596–1648			
Charles IX 1604–11				
				Elector John Sigismund 1608–19
Gustavus Adolphus 1611–32			Michael Romanov 1613–45	Elector George William 1619–40
Christina 1632–54		Ladislas 1632–48		Elector Frederick William 1640–88
			Alexis 1645–76	
	Frederick III 1648–70	John Casimir 1648–68		
Charles X 1654–60				
Charles XI 1660–97				
		Michael Wisnowieski 1669–73		
	Christian V 1670–99	John Sobieski 1674–96		
			Feodor 1676–82	
			Ivan & Peter (Regent Sophia) 1682–9	
			Peter I 1689–1725	Elector Frederick III 1688–1701
Charles XII 1697–1718	Frederick IV 1699–1730	Augustus II 1697–1733		who became King Frederick I in Prussia from 1701–13
				King Frederick William I 1713–40

Appendix II

The House of Vasa in Sweden and Poland

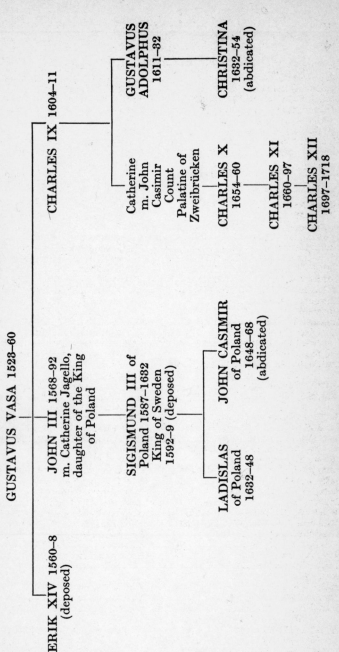

GUSTAVUS VASA 1528–60

ERIK XIV 1560–8 (deposed)

JOHN III 1568–92
m. Catherine Jagello,
daughter of the King
of Poland

CHARLES IX 1604–11

SIGISMUND III of
Poland 1587–1632
King of Sweden
1592–9 (deposed)

GUSTAVUS
ADOLPHUS
1611–32

Catherine
m. John
Casimir
Count
Palatine of
Zweibrücken

CHRISTINA
1632–54
(abdicated)

CHARLES X
1654–60

LADISLAS
of Poland
1632–48

JOHN CASIMIR
of Poland
1648–68
(abdicated)

CHARLES XI
1660–97

CHARLES XII
1697–1718

Index